DOMINION MANDATE

Fulfilling Your Divine Purpose In The Marketplace

AKIN THOMAS

Copyright © 2024 Akin Thomas

ALL RIGHTS RESERVED. No part of this book may be reproduced or transmitted in any form whatsoever, electronic or mechanical, including photocopying, recording, or by any informational storage or retrieval system without the express written, dated, and signed permission from the author.

Title: Dominion Mandate: Fulfilling divine purpose in the marketplace

ISBN: 978-1-0686737-9-5

Category: Personal Development/Business/Spiritual

Publisher: Breakfree Forever Publishing (a trading name for Breakfree Forever Consultancy Ltd)

Scripture References

Unless otherwise indicated, Scripture quotations are taken from the New King James Version®. Copyright © 1982 by Thomas Nelson. Used by permission. All rights reserved.

LIMITS OF LIABILITY/DISCLAIMER OF WARRANTY: The author and publisher of this book have used their best efforts in preparing this material. The author and publisher make no representation or warranties with respect to the accuracy, applicability, or completeness of the contents. They disclaim any warranties (expressed or implied), or merchantability for any particular purpose. The author and publisher shall in no event be held liable for any loss or other damages, including but not limited to special, incidental, consequential, or other damages.

The information presented in this publication is compiled from sources believed to be accurate. However, the publisher assumes no responsibility for errors or omissions. The information in this publication is not intended to replace or substitute professional advice. The author and publisher specifically disclaim any liability, loss, or risk that is incurred as a consequence, directly or indirectly, of the use and application of any of the contents of this work.

Printed in the United Kingdom.

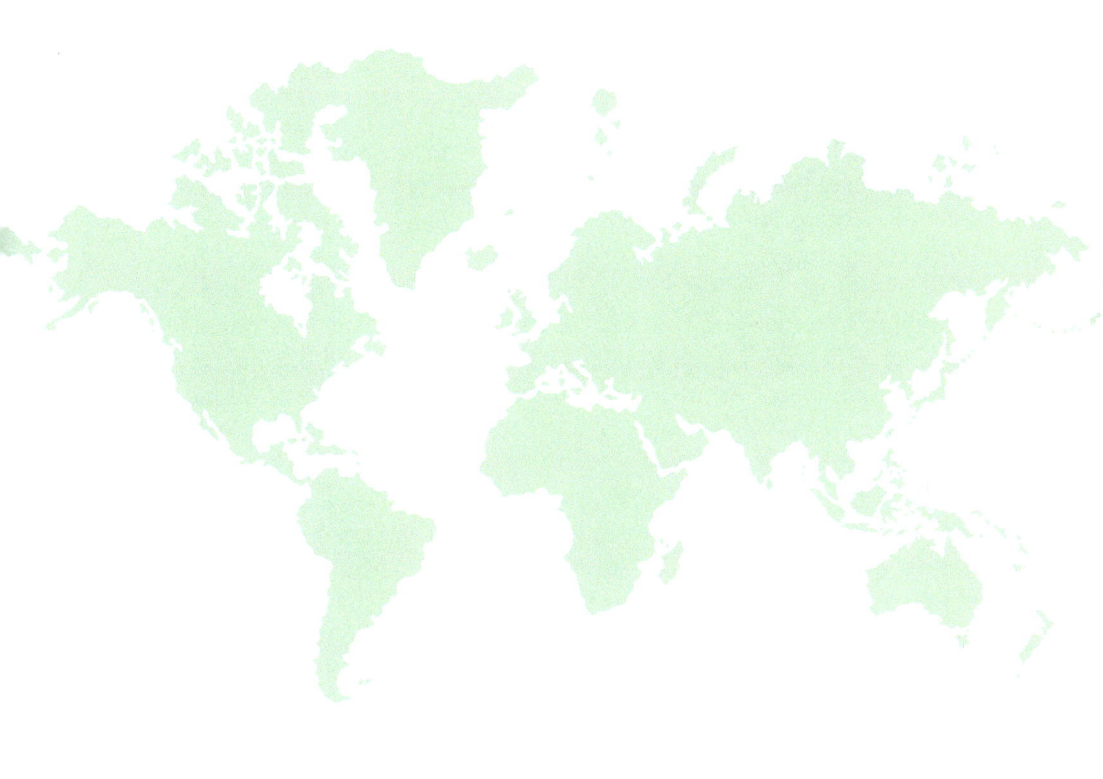

DEDICATION

Before I mention anyone else, I need to give thanks to my heavenly Father. You gave this to me, Lord. I'm a merely a steward, but I thank You for trusting me, even when I wasn't trustworthy. It is a privilege to know that I've done something truly inspired by you.

There are so many people who have been part of this journey, too many to mention. But there are some people who have walked with me and allowed me to teach, mentor and encourage on this Dominion Mandate journey. They have been part of a group who met every two weeks and have helped to shape what I'm sharing with you.

We have prayed together, fought together, won together. We have been vulnerable and have shared truths which go beyond our cashflow! Each of them has taken their enterprise – most of them from an idea – and they have grown in confidence and stature.

Leighsa, Juliet, Verona, Ben, Debbie, Deborah, Joseph, Amede, Bimpe, Olivia-Zara, Chisom, Chelena, I want to thank you for trusting me. Pastor Davis and Joselyn, you encouraged me every step of the way. You have been an incredible blessing to me.

Special mention to Sheyi and Shola, my incredible children who are amazing Kingdom entrepreneurs, who have come from out of my shadow and now shine in ways that make me so proud. And my wife Denise, thank you for being so faithful and supportive. Thank you for not giving up, for not walking away when at times it would have been easier for you do so. I can do what I do because of you. This I especially dedicate to you.

CONTENTS

INTRODUCTION	1
I HAD TO LEARN THE HARD WAY	3
WHAT IS THE DOMINION MANDATE?	7
GET THE FOUNDATIONS RIGHT	9
STEWARDSHIP	11
THE SIX DM CIRCLES	19
NURTURING RELATIONSHIP WITH GOD	21
DEVELOPING CHARACTER: FOUR SPIRITUAL MUSCLES	31
DEVELOPING CHARACTER: THE OTHER THREE SPIRITUAL MUSCLES	45
FULFILLING PURPOSE	51
BUILDING A POWERFUL TEAM	53
DEVELOPING GREAT SYSTEMS	59
SEEKING A DIVINELY INSPIRED SOLUTION	63
POSSESSING MEANS DISPOSSESSING	65
RELATIONSHIP WITH MONEY	75
TAKE CARE OF YOURSELF	87
EXIT STRATEGY: BEWARE	91
FINAL THOUGHTS	93

DOMINION MANDATE

INTRODUCTION

This book aims to equip leaders to operate at their best in the marketplace, to glorify our Heavenly Father.

The Dominion Mandate must be rooted in God's Word. Anything less would lead you astray. Scripture will be woven throughout the book, often repeated, as it is multi-dimensional. It's crucial to dissect the Word to broaden our understanding of its application.

Please, adopt a Berean spirit and verify the Scriptures yourself. Explore the context, cross-reference, and ensure you're confident in applying God's Word for market dominance.

>
>
> *'These were more fair-minded than those in Thessalonica, in that they received the word with all readiness, and searched the Scriptures daily to find out whether these things were so.'*
>
> **Acts 17:11**

Throughout this book, the default version for quoting Scriptures will be the New King James Version (NKJV). Where other Bible versions have been used, these will be noted accordingly.

▶ Why I wrote this book

Ever since I've been walking with Jesus Christ as my Lord and Saviour, I've been operating in the marketplace. I've started up many different ventures, thinking I was smart, deluding myself about achievements, justifying mediocrity. But God gave me the Dominion Mandate many years ago. I would pick it up, put it down, talk big, and act small. It frustrated me and yet excited me. But to be truthful, I didn't really know what to do with it.

When I became a member of ARC in South London, this burning passion to I felt a calling to work with business owners and entrepreneurs, so I started a ministry for those at the beginning of their journey or unsure of how to start. We met every other Saturday, and each session was God-inspired and Holy Spirit-led. The group grew into a strong support system, helping each other and approaching business in a truly divine way.

In June 2024, our church started a series called Advance, based on Deuteronomy 1:6–8, which stirred something in me. While teaching and preaching on Advance, I felt God speaking to me. Then, on July 27th, 2024, God woke me up at 4am, guiding me to purchase the domain www.dominion-mandate.com and follow His instructions to design a game, write a book, and coach Christians on leading and having dominion in the marketplace.

This book is my obedience to that calling. At first, I struggled with how to write it, unsure if sharing my story would seem egotistical. But God instructed me to use it, knowing it would resonate and encourage others. So, I share my journey, trusting it will inspire you.

How to use this book

The best way to use this book is to ask yourself, "Am I truly operating in the marketplace as God intends?" If the answer is no, use this book as a reference. Think of it as a check-up to assess your leadership, vision, strategy, and products, and see how you can align them with God's Word.

I was inspired to write this book, and I believe it will help you. As I write, it's helping me align as well. This isn't a one-size-fits-all guide, as God's plans for you are unique, but His principles remain constant.

I HAD TO LEARN THE HARD WAY

> 'Do not fret because of evildoers, nor be envious of the workers of iniquity.
>
> For they shall soon be cut down like the grass, and wither as the green herb.
>
> Trust in the Lord, and do good; dwell in the land, and feed on His faithfulness.
>
> Delight yourself also in the Lord, and He shall give you the desires of your heart. Commit your way to the Lord, trust also in Him, and He shall bring it to pass.
>
> He shall bring forth your righteousness as the light, and your justice as the noonday.
>
> 'Rest in the Lord, and wait patiently for Him; do not fret because of him who prospers in his way, because of the man who brings wicked schemes to pass. Cease from anger, and forsake wrath; do not fret—it only causes harm.
>
> For evildoers shall be cut off; but those who wait on the Lord, they shall inherit the earth.
>
> 'For yet a little while and the wicked shall be no more; Indeed, you will look carefully for his place, but it shall be no more. But the meek shall inherit the earth, and shall delight themselves in the abundance of peace.'
>
> **Psalm 37:1–11**

I learned the hard way. Over nearly 30 years in the marketplace, I've experienced highs and lows. My Nigerian roots fueled my passion for entrepreneurship, but for years, I was driven by worldly motivations. I justified chasing wealth by calling it God's blessings, both before and after finding Christ.

But then one day it all came crashing down.

I was driven by success, equating it to making money. As the youngest in a senior leadership role in local government, I was on track to become Assistant Director but realized working for others wouldn't fulfill my ambitions. In 1997, during an Action Learning Set, I had an epiphany, decided to quit, and informed my director on the spot—without even telling my wife. Thirty days later, with no severance, I sat at home thinking, "What have I done?!"

Now, I wasn't without a parachute, because I was a hustler. I had been involved in property and in renovations, and then in selling. But this didn't necessarily give me the cashflow I needed.

I remember sitting in my house for 30 days, with no income, and then I received a call from a former colleague, asking me to come and help him. This was the beginning of my consultancy journey.

I dreamed of becoming a property millionaire and retiring at 40, but God had other plans. While my property business grew steadily, I craved more and joined developers with far greater resources. For a while, I kept up, but I was chasing the wrong things—living a champagne lifestyle on lemonade money.

This made me strive even more to be successful.

I unknowingly got involved in a Ponzi scheme, seduced by greed without realizing it. I'd invest money on Monday and receive unbelievable returns—25–30%—by Thursday. Starting small, I gradually increased the amounts and even involved family, friends, and church members, wanting to share the "good fortune." They trusted me as I brought them impressive returns.

The property business was thriving, but I saw an opportunity to accelerate growth by diverting funds into investments and using the returns to expand. Some may call it foolish, but these were polished people with Mayfair offices, complex deals, and lavish hospitality. When I requested paperwork, I was met with a wad of cash, so I overlooked tying up loose ends.

I had involved 20–30 people, and everyone was earning and reinvesting. But soon, things shifted—communication dwindled, calls went unanswered, and retrieving money became a struggle, coming back in small amounts with endless excuses. Frustrated, I still didn't stop.

I once had £40,000 in our home safe and told my wife, "One last roll, then we're done." She warned me not to, sensing something was wrong, but I didn't listen. Soon, everyone vanished, communication stopped, and £1.5 million of people's money was gone.

My world changed forever, though I only thank God now. Desperate to repay everyone, I sold everything, including my property portfolio, but it wasn't enough. Some investors, angered by their losses, even hired someone to take me out.

I never imagined sitting with my wife in a room of intimidating men who knew my kids' names, schools, and bank details. Their ultimatum: "Get the money." Desperate, I scrambled to repay everyone but delayed paying HMRC. They didn't wait and filed bankruptcy against me.

At my first hearing, the compassionate judge urged me to find a solution and adjourned for time. As a hustler, I had handled many challenges, but this time I knew I had to surrender. My home, with subsidence and no insurance, was worthless and unsellable.

On May 9th, 2012, I was declared bankrupt at the High Court. Two days later, I flew to Detroit for Holy Convocation, my head spinning as I tried to stay composed. The Scripture for the gathering's theme was:

> *'For You, O God, have tested us; You have refined us as silver is refined.
> You brought us into the net; You laid affliction on our backs.
> You have caused men to ride over our heads; we went through fire and through water; but You brought us out to rich fulfilment.'*
> **Psalm 66:10–12**

A few weeks after returning to the UK, we lost our home, going from a 4-bedroom house with two cars to a small, windowless room in Brixton. I had hit rock bottom and dragged my family down with me. Now, I see it was part of God's plan to use me in the marketplace for His glory.

DOMINION MANDATE

WHAT IS THE DOMINION MANDATE?

The Dominion Mandate is a divinely given instruction to us. The Dominion Mandate is uttered in the first words God spoke to man:

> *'Then God said, "Let Us make man in Our image, according to Our likeness; let them have dominion over the fish of the sea, over the birds of the air, and over the cattle, over all the earth and over every creeping thing that creeps on the earth." So God created man in His own image; in the image of God He created him; male and female He created them. Then God blessed them, and God said to them, "Be fruitful and multiply; fill the earth and subdue it; have dominion over the fish of the sea, over the birds of the air, and over every living thing that moves on the earth."'*
>
> ***Genesis 1:26–28***

The Dominion Mandate is about using the power and influence God has given you to excel in the marketplace and reflect His glory. The Hebrew word for dominion, *radah* (raw-dah), means to subjugate or rule over. Business leaders, take note of verse 28, which outlines a divine strategy: "Be fruitful and multiply, fill the earth and subdue it"—we'll explore this further in upcoming chapters.

A mandate is an authoritative command, meaning the person receiving it has the responsibility and authority to carry out a specific task. It's not a suggestion, but a direct instruction.

We've been given a divine instruction to rule and dominate our territories, whether that's a village, city, or nation. Today, our reach is limitless, and to dominate means taking authority in a world that opposes Christ. The Dominion Mandate is about using God's authority to succeed in the marketplace for His glory, keeping Him central in all our actions.

Deuteronomy 8:18 reminds us that God gives us power to create wealth to establish His covenant, not just for personal gain. To fulfill the Dominion Mandate, we must follow His Word, not just what's convenient.

DOMINION
MANDATE

GET THE FOUNDATIONS RIGHT

I want to ensure that we are aligned on the foundations of the Dominion Mandate. There is no theological debate involved; it's simply setting out core Kingdom principles that this book is built on.

▶ Soul-winning vehicle

At the core of every Kingdom business and enterprise is that it is a soul-winning vehicle. If you don't believe in this statement, I suggest you stop reading.

> *'And Jesus came and spoke to them, saying, "All authority has been given to Me in heaven and on earth. Go therefore and make disciples of all the nations, baptising them in the name of the Father and of the Son and of the Holy Spirit, teaching them to observe all things that I have commanded you; and lo, I am with you always, even to the end of the age." Amen.'*
>
> **Matthew 28:18–20**

Some of you will ask what has the Great Commission got to do with how you operate in the market. The answer is everything. The Dominion Mandate is about Christ and about souls. We are uniquely positioned to have impact on thousands of people – our staff, our customers, our suppliers. We must use our **influence for God's glory.**

▶ You were created to have dominion

We were created to have dominion. These are the first words spoken to man and that should make us sit up and pay attention. Dominion over the earth, though, never another person. Dominion should also relate to an industry. You were not created to just survive or settle; you were created to have dominion. God spoke it into our DNA.

▶ Shine to give God glory

> *"'Let your light so shine before men, that they may see your good works and glorify your Father in heaven.'"*
>
> **Matthew 5:16**

This type of 'shine' is way beyond your natural capacity. There are things you can do because of the skills and intellect that can be ascribed to you. They could be good – or even great – skills, but people will try to ascribe the glory to you. And you will know "This isn't it." The type of shine spoken of here is one so bright that people will look at you and conclude it could only be God – believers and, more importantly, unbelievers. Some through gritted teeth will have to confess God must have done it.

Surely the place where this type of shine has most impact is in the marketplace. This type of shine shouldn't be confined to church on a Sunday; you are talking to the converted there. But, in the marketplace, you have a visibility and audience that are expansive. You have eyes on you that you won't even know about – especially with the digital reach we have. I go back to a fundamental we spoke about earlier: your business must be a soul-winning machine. How? By shining!

▶ A lifestyle not just for Sunday

Why do many business owners raise holy hands on Sundays but are unrecognisable for the rest of the week? Which character in Scripture did you see switching on and switching off? Your walk with Christ must show up in everything you do. The walk is seven days a week, 365. Sunday Christians cannot achieve the Mandate. The chapter on character will open this up in more detail.

▶ An excellent spirit

Everything we do should honour God. Our endeavours should be done with an excellent spirit – the service you provide, the way in which you treat your customers, the décor of your office/shop. It should all speak of excellence. It doesn't mean you will have the most palatial spaces, but the heart and intent in which you do everything should be excellent.

STEWARDSHIP

Although stewardship is foundational, it is worthy of a separate chapter. Without understanding you are a steward, everything else is amiss. And what's interesting is that whenever I have conversations with so many entrepreneurs or business leaders, there is a lot of pause and reflection. For many, stewardship has been absent.

> *'Therefore David blessed the Lord before all the assembly; and David said: "Blessed are You, Lord God of Israel, our Father, forever and ever.*
> *Yours, O Lord, is the greatness, the power and the glory, the victory and the majesty; for all that is in heaven and in earth is Yours; Yours is the Kingdom, O Lord, and You are exalted as head over all.*
>
> *"Both riches and honour come from You, and You reign over all. In Your hand is power and might; in Your hand it is to make great and to give strength to all. Now therefore, our God, we thank You and praise Your glorious name.*
> *But who am I, and who are my people, that we should be able to offer so willingly as this? For all things come from You, And of Your own we have given You. For we are aliens and pilgrims before You, As were all our fathers; Our days on earth are as a shadow, And without hope.*
>
> *"O Lord our God, all this abundance that we have prepared to build You a house for Your holy name is from Your hand, and is all Your own. I know also, my God, that You test the heart and have pleasure in uprightness. As for me, in the uprightness of my heart I have willingly offered all these things; and now with joy I have seen Your people, who are present here to offer willingly to You."'*
>
> ***1 Chronicles 29:10–17***

David understood he was a steward. So, what is stewardship? **Stewardship is where you have been given delegated authority to take care of possessions on behalf of another, normally a higher authority.** God has delegated authority for us to take care of this planet in its entirety on His behalf. This includes the business or idea that you have.

There are principles of stewardship we must learn, understand, and then apply, in order for us to be true disciples of God. These principles are counterintuitive to what the world will tell you, so you must be transformed by the renewing of your mind. God's principles are not the world's principles. The world will take some of God's principles and twist them and manipulate them. This is why sometimes it looks like there are grey areas, but your job is to understand what God says, by studying the Scriptures and then applying them as God intended.

Stewardship has five principles.

▶ Principle 1: It's not yours

> 'The earth is the Lord's, and all its fullness,
> The world and those who dwell therein.'
>
> ***Psalm 24:1 (NKJV)***
>
> 'The earth is the Lord's, and everything in it.
> The world and all its people belong to Him.'
>
> ***Psalm 24:1 (NLT)***

Nothing is yours. We have been gifted these things for a season. My business isn't mine; my children are not mine; my house isn't mine. They are God's, but He has been gracious enough to allow us to possess.

> 'The heaven, even the heavens, are the Lord's; but the earth He has given to the children of men.'
>
> ***Psalm 115:16***

'What is man that You are mindful of him, and the son of man that You visit him? For You have made him a little lower than the angels, and You have crowned him with glory and honour. You have made him to have dominion over the works of Your hands; You have put all things under his feet...'

Psalm 8:4–6

We must readjust how we see ownership. It's not yours, it's God's. Therefore, you have to shift your language from 'my' business to 'His' business, 'my' ideas to 'His' ideas. For some of us, this is a major shift and means you are going to have totally rethink your relationship with that enterprise you run – whether you have two employees or 2,000. It belongs to God. This is an ego-busting principle. But if you think about it, it's also a liberating principle. It's God's and He knows what He wants from it.

Think about the vocabulary of the world – 'self-made millionaire', they did it 'by themselves', etc. These are lies and ones we should never repeat. Psalm 8:6 should underpin our thinking: 'You have made him to have dominion over the works of Your hands; You have put all things under his feet…', You must acknowledge that God chose you to operate this business on His behalf. God has entrusted you with a gift. How do you ensure that you never allow the world to lull you into a false sense of success or a false sense of failure? **Let go and let God.**

Principle 2: You are responsible for what God gives you

> 'Then the Lord God took the man and put him in the garden of Eden to tend and keep it.'
>
> ***Genesis 2:15***
>
> 'And that servant who knew his master's will, and did not prepare himself or do according to his will, shall be beaten with many stripes. But he who did not know, yet committed things deserving of stripes, shall be beaten with few. For everyone to whom much is given, from him much will be required; and to whom much has been committed, of him they will ask the more.'
>
> ***Luke 12:47–48***

To be responsible suggests we should understand what we have been given to take care of. But the truth is often we don't; we are ignorant of what God has given us. When we are ignorant, we are likely to misuse what we've been given. However, when we become clear on what we have and the value of what's been given to us, we should then begin to use the thing correctly.

HOWEVER… if you continue to undervalue or misappropriate what you've been given, it's no longer misuse (out of ignorance), it becomes abuse (because you are cognisant). A quick example: You work seven days a week, you learn through teaching that the Sabbath is holy and a day of rest. If you cease to work on the Sabbath and rest, you use the Sabbath correctly. But, if you continue to work – knowing fully well it is a day of rest – it's now abuse. A steward must always understand and value what they have. This is the starting rung of being responsible.

When God gives you a business idea to launch and take to market, He's saying He trusts you. Does our conduct inform God that His trust in us is well placed?

▶ Principle 3: You have to be accountable

> *'Now after a long time the master of those servants returned and settled accounts with them. And the one who had received the five talents came and brought him five more, saying, "Master, you entrusted to me five talents. See, I have [made a profit and] gained five more talents."'*
> **Matthew 25:19–20 (AMP)**

I want you to pause for a moment and imagine you're in a room with a table and two chairs. You are sitting in one chair and waiting. You hear footsteps getting louder and the door opens. God enters the room, carrying a file. God sits down opposite you and starts to flick through the file. He looks up at you for a moment and then continues to read. He then sits back, pauses, and asks: "What did you do with all I gave you?"

We are all going to have to give an account, and God isn't going to take anything off the table for our convenience.

So, you took your company to a £10m turnover, but you never prayed with your children, because you were too busy! You cut corners, because it was easier. You squandered what He gave you on material things. You're going to have to give an account!

We are stewarding everything we have responsibility for, and so we are going to have an account for all those things. In what areas of your life are you failing to be accountable?

Principle 4: You must add value

> *"'Then he who had received the one talent came and said, 'Lord, I knew you to be a hard man, reaping where you have not sown, and gathering where you have not scattered seed. And I was afraid, and went and hid your talent in the ground. Look, there you have what is yours.' But his lord answered and said to him, "You wicked and lazy servant, you knew that I reap where I have not sown, and gather where I have not scattered seed. So you ought to have deposited my money with the bankers, and at my coming I would have received back my own with interest. So take the talent from him, and give it to him who has ten talents.' For to everyone who has, more will be given, and he will have abundance; but from him who does not have, even what he has will be taken away."'*
>
> *Matthew 25:24–30*

For me, the most exciting but also most scary bit of being a steward – especially as entrepreneurs and business leaders – is adding value. Truthfully, many people in business are taking value, but not adding value. If you were to have an honest audit of the people you employ, how many of them are truly adding value?

Unfortunately, many are taking a lot and giving little back. But let's also look in the mirror. There is an assumption that, because we are leaders and entrepreneurs, by default we are adding value. But that is not necessarily true. What value have you added to your staff? (Do they know you love Jesus?) How do your customers feel when they interact with your business? How have you helped one of your suppliers, when you didn't have to?

We tend to think about adding in big ways, but the true essence of adding value is most powerful in the small things. A few examples include knowing the name of your cleaner and stopping to have a conversation with him/her; leaving rented accommodation in a better condition than when you first occupied it; having a policy that no member of your staff should need to use a food bank… We have the privilege of being able to add value that can amplify God's glory.

▶ Principle 5: There is a reward

'"His lord said to him, 'Well done, good and faithful servant; you were faithful over a few things, I will make you ruler over many things. Enter into the joy of your lord.'"'

Matthew 25:21

'"For to everyone who has, more will be given, and he will have abundance; but from him who does not have, even what he has will be taken away."'

Matthew 25:29

'So Jesus answered and said, "Assuredly, I say to you, there is no one who has left house or brothers or sisters or father or mother or wife or children or lands, for My sake and the Gospel's, who shall not receive a hundredfold now in this time –houses and brothers and sisters and mothers and children and lands, with persecutions – and in the age to come, eternal life."'
Mark 10:29–30

A note of caution: In Scripture, no one we admire chased the reward; it was freely given. For those who chased the reward, e.g. Gehazi in 2 Kings 5, it didn't end well. Don't chase the reward, allow God to bless you in His own time. Sometimes we are too quick to chase the reward in terms of material comforts. It's cool to have nice things, but don't go and acquire before it is time. Really seek God and, if we truly trust Him, He will bring these things to us. Matthew 6:33 is explicit: "…all these things will be added unto you!"

DOMINION MANDATE

THE SIX DM CIRCLES

There are six circles of the Dominion Mandate:

- Nurturing relationship with God
- Developing your character
- Fulfilling your purpose
- Building a powerful team
- Developing great systems
- Seeking a divinely-inspired solution

The first three (nurturing relationship, developing your character, fulfilling your purpose) are internal, and very personal to you as an individual.

The latter three (building a powerful team, developing great systems, seeking a divinely-inspired-inspired solution) are external, and really an expression of how your enterprise or business will function in the marketplace. Although all six elements are important, I want to put weight on the inner three, because they are the enablers for the outer three.

We will explore each of the circles in a separate chapter. I encourage you to take your time; reflect on what you are reading; have honest conversations with yourself – and with others – and be intentional about the changes you have to make. We will provide some exercises or checklists that will help you.

DOMINION
MANDATE

NURTURING RELATIONSHIP WITH GOD

This is fundamental to everything; it's your very being. I want to start with Jabez:

> *'Jabez was more honourable than his brothers. His mother had named him Jabez, saying, "I gave birth to him in pain." Jabez cried out to the God of Israel, "Oh, that You would bless me and enlarge my territory! Let Your hand be with me, and keep me from harm so that I will be free from pain." And God granted his request.'*
>
> **1 Chronicles 4:9–10**

Jabez is mentioned in only two verses and then disappears, but the impact of his prayer is profound, and I argue it was because of the relationship Jabez had nurtured with God. God wasn't going to just grant this request to a random stranger. This is the prayer of a man who had an intimate relationship with God.

Our relationship with God should be our priority – everything flows from this. However, many of us struggle with the very thing that shapes who we are and, more importantly, who we have been predestined to be.

Many of us use earthly relationships (e.g. with our parents) as a blueprint for our spiritual relationship with God. Often this leads us into wrong thinking and warps our relationship into being transactional, superficial or inconsistent. So I want us to pause and get back to important basics.

The Bible is a love affair in which God wants to reconcile Himself with His people so that He is able to truly express His love to His people. And He was willing to pay a high price to achieve this.

> *'For God so loved the world that He gave His only begotten Son, that whoever believes in Him should not perish but have everlasting life. For God did not send His Son into the world to condemn the world, but that the world through Him might be saved.'*
>
> **John 3:16–17**

Love is an intimate experience.

▶ David is a template we can all learn from

If there is a case study for nurturing relationship with God, David is right up there, and we could dedicate a whole book on him. But let's look at some key features…

> *'But now your kingdom shall not continue. The Lord has sought for Himself a man after His own heart, and the Lord has commanded him to be commander over His people, because you have not kept what the Lord commanded you.'*
>
> **1 Samuel 13:14**
>
> *'And when He had removed him, He raised up for them David as king, to whom also He gave testimony and said, "I have found David the son of Jesse, a man after My own heart, who will do all My will."'*
>
> **Acts 13:22**

The Old and New Testaments confirm that David is the only man who has the privilege of being called "a man after My own heart." But in Acts, note that it says of David "who will do all My will." That provides a deep understanding of David, willing to do all God's will.

There are so many examples that give us insight into the deep relationship David had with God. I want to use the following to help us to nurture our relationship with God.

David's reverence for God is epitomised in his relationship with King Saul. Saul had despised him from the time they had returned from war and the women sang and danced for David singing: "Saul has slain his thousands, and David his tens of thousands" (1 Samuel 18:7).

This jealousy turned into a murderous rage and, on multiple occasions, Saul sought to kill David. Just imagine if you had been given the opportunity to take revenge…

> *'Then the men of David said to him, "This is the day of which the Lord said to you, 'Behold, I will deliver your enemy into your hand, that you may do to him as it seems good to you.'" And David arose and secretly cut off a corner of Saul's robe. Now it happened afterward that David's heart troubled him because he had cut Saul's robe. And he said to his men, "The Lord forbid that I should do this thing to my master, the Lord's anointed, to stretch out my hand against him, seeing he is the anointed of the Lord." So David restrained his servants with these words, and did not allow them to rise against Saul. And Saul got up from the cave and went on his way.'*
>
> **1 Samuel 24:4–7**

Would you have listened to those around you who had a completely rational case to take revenge? Or could you go beyond your emotions, as David did? In fact, on the second occasion when David spares Saul's life, he refers to him as 'father'!

David constantly sought the Lord for guidance. In 1 Samuel 30, when he and his men returned to Ziklag from an operation, they found the place burnt down and their wives and children taken. His own turned on him and spoke of stoning him. How did David respond?

>
> *'Then David said to Abiathar the priest, Ahimelech's son, "Please bring the ephod here to me." And Abiathar brought the ephod to David. So David inquired of the Lord, saying, "Shall I pursue this troop? Shall I overtake them?"*
> *And He answered him, "Pursue, for you shall surely overtake them and without fail recover all."'*
>
> **1 Samuel 30:7–8**

When David was backed into a corner and there looked like there was no hope, he enquired of the Lord and the Lord responded. Why? Because of relationship.

But as we know, this is a man who was far from perfect: he's lied, committed adultery, and sanctioned murder.

The story of David and Bathsheba illustrates David at his worst and his best. At his worst, in that he sleeps with Bathsheba, the wife of Uriah, gets her pregnant, then tries to cover his sin by calling Uriah back from the frontline to sleep with his wife, which Uriah refuses to do out of loyalty to David and his fellow soldiers. So David orders his murder on the battlefield to cover up his sin.

In 2 Samuel 16, Nathan confronts David with a scenario. David is so indignant about what he has been told, until Nathan challenges him to look in the mirror, because the perpetrator is David himself. But David, unlike his predecessor Saul, doesn't look to blame anyone. He simply responds: "I have sinned against the Lord."

The Lord relents on all He was going to do, but indeed the child dies. Even this shows the deepness of David's relationship with God, confounding all his servants:

> 'When David saw that his servants were whispering, David perceived that the child was dead. Therefore David said to his servants, "Is the child dead?" And they said, "He is dead."
>
> 'So David arose from the ground, washed and anointed himself, and changed his clothes; and he went into the house of the Lord and worshipped. Then he went to his own house; and when he requested, they set food before him, and he ate. Then his servants said to him, "What is this that you have done? You fasted and wept for the child while he was alive, but when the child died, you arose and ate food."
>
> 'And he said, "While the child was alive, I fasted and wept; for I said, 'Who can tell whether the Lord will be gracious to me, that the child may live?' But now he is dead; why should I fast? Can I bring him back again? I shall go to him, but he shall not return to me."'
>
> ***2 Samuel 12:19–23***

After an excruciatingly painful experience, his first response was to worship! And it gets deeper. From this experience, David writes Psalm 51 – the most incredible prayer of repentance.

So a deeply flawed character, and yet the statement by God stands firm. David messed up big, but always sought the presence of God. Whenever we look in the mirror we will probably see a deeply flawed, even messed-up character, but this means we qualify if we seek to have a deep passion for God.

Remember, we are not perfect, but we are perfecting; this is bound in our relationship with God. So let's highlight some key things for nurturing our relationship with God.

▶ Prioritise your time with God

Pray – and not just when it's convenient for you – but let your prayer be sacrificial. The Word talks about those who diligently seek God. Being diligent requires a determination and urgency. Diligence also points to first and early. Wake up early and pray. If you can work 14-hour days, you can find the discipline to pray. I say the most important board meeting you should have is on your knees daily with your heavenly Father. And you can bring every aspect of your business venture to God, but be careful, there is much more to life than the business – your friends, your family, your church community.

Are you praying for God's hand or His presence? Honour the Provider more than His provision. And, most importantly, pray about how your enterprise can be a soul-winning vehicle.

▶ Study the Word

I emphasise study, because reading is good, but it's not enough. Every answer to every problem lies in Scripture. Everything you are going to encounter in your business, the Scriptures have the answer. God has given you a business manual, but to optimise it, you need to study. Make Bible studies a priority, because God's Word is the key to unlock everything you need and must fulfil. It will show you how to conduct yourself; how not to worry; how to be honest; how to handle money; how to treat your staff; how to handle disputes; how to tackle your enemies; how to show love….

▶ Fasting

> *'And when He had come into the house, His disciples asked Him privately, "Why could we not cast it out?" So He said to them, "This kind can come out by nothing but prayer and fasting."'*
>
> **Mark 9:28–29**

There are some challenges you will encounter that can only be overcome by prayer AND fasting. This shows us the power of fasting, and yet it is one of the most neglected and underutilised tools that Father has given us. And when we do cover our mouths, often we are dieting and not actually fasting. Fasting is covering our mouths and abstaining for a purpose. You may want to hear from Father and know you need to go deeper. You may have a big challenge, so fast. The Word is littered with examples of how fasting was the catalyst for great exploits in Scripture.

> *'And Mordecai told them to answer Esther: "Do not think in your heart that you will escape in the king's palace any more than all the other Jews. For if you remain completely silent at this time, relief and deliverance will arise for the Jews from another place, but you and your father's house will perish. Yet who knows whether you have come to the kingdom for such a time as this?"*
>
> *Then Esther told them to reply to Mordecai: "Go, gather all the Jews who are present in Shushan, and fast for me; neither eat nor drink for three days, night or day. My maids and I will fast likewise. And so I will go to the king, which is against the law; and if I perish, I perish!"'*
>
> **Esther 4:13–16**

Many of us are very familiar with what Mordecai says to Esther: "Yet who knows whether you have come to the kingdom for such a time as this?" It is a pronouncement of purpose and a mandate that must be fulfilled. As Christians, we tend to use this to encourage others – and rightly so – but equally important was Esther's response: "Fast for me and I will do likewise."

Just for clarity, fasting social media or not watching your favourite TV programme is sacrificial, but it's not fasting. Fasting is a physical, mental and spiritual experience. When you cover your mouth, you need to be dedicating real time with God. Use the time when you would have had lunch to find that secret place to pray or read Scriptures. Dedicate that time, because God will meet you in those spaces and give you the answers you seek.

And finally, you may corporately fast, but when fasting individually, no one needs to know.

'"Moreover, when you fast, do not be like the hypocrites, with a sad countenance. For they disfigure their faces that they may appear to men to be fasting. Assuredly, I say to you, they have their reward. But you, when you fast, anoint your head and wash your face, so that you do not appear to men to be fasting, but to your Father who is in the secret place; and your Father who sees in secret will reward you openly."'

Matthew 6:16–18

Fasting is about you and God. Give it the reverence it deserves.

▶ Your closest companion – the Holy Spirit

'"If you love Me, keep My commandments. And I will pray the Father, and He will give you another Helper, that He may abide with you forever – the Spirit of truth, whom the world cannot receive, because it neither sees Him nor knows Him; but you know Him, for He dwells with you and will be in you."'

John 14:15–17

'"But the Helper, the Holy Spirit, whom the Father will send in My name, He will teach you all things, and bring to your remembrance all things that I said to you."'

John 14:26

Nurturing your relationship with God means developing an intimate relationship with the Holy Spirit. Jesus told us that He will give us another Helper, one the world cannot receive, but we know Him, because He dwells with us and in us.

Jesus went onto say He will teach us ALL things and bring to our remembrance all things He has taught us.

The Holy Spirit isn't our companion just on Sundays and during prayer times; He is our constant, always with us, always available, always ready to help. And yet we neglect Him, making decisions without Him, thinking we know best. A key way we will stand out as Christian business leaders and entrepreneurs is allowing the Holy Spirit to lead us and help us.

> *'"But you shall receive power when the Holy Spirit has come upon you; and you shall be witnesses to Me in Jerusalem, and in all Judea and Samaria, and to the end of the earth."'*
>
> **Acts 1:8**

This point is incredibly important: the Holy Spirit gives us power. That means the Holy Spirit gives us something that we don't have. We need to understand the delusion many of us walk around with: having a sense of power. You may believe you're powerful, but what is the source of that power? The Holy Spirit gives you incredible access to do things, which you cannot do yourself. We must ensure we use the power correctly, to be a witness of Jesus Christ, our Lord and Saviour.

And He's available to all of us. It's not complex. As we accepted the invitation to receive Jesus as our LORD and Saviour, we were given automatic access to the Holy Spirit. So commune with Him. Talk with Him, ask Him questions about every aspect of your enterprise. But it requires going deep, taking time, not trying to use Him like a genie out of a bottle, but cultivating a genuine relationship, which will take time to mature.

When you do, you will hear things, see things and know things the world has no access to. So just pause and ask yourself why, if you have such an advantage of being part of God's Kingdom, are you watching and copying people of the world and how they operate?

▶ Faith is your fuel

'But without faith it is impossible to please Him, for he who comes to God must believe that He is, and that He is a rewarder of those who diligently seek Him.'

Hebrews 11:6

If God has mandated you to have dominion in the marketplace, your fuel is going to be faith. God is going to speak to you and show you things way beyond your natural capacity. They won't make sense; they'll be contrary to what you are experiencing and, for many of us, they'll scare us! But faith is what's going to keep you in the game. The world gives us logical equations for business and therefore if it doesn't fit within a formula, the world tells us it won't work. But we are in the world but not of the world.

I remember a time when our company had NO money coming in and bills pouring out. I remember telling my finance manager (who was a Muslim) to have faith, and he shouted back: "Faith doesn't pay bills!" A few months later, when God provided incredibly, he was almost dancing on the table!

And there will be times when you will wrestle between fear and faith. You are human and the mandate could be overwhelming. Please don't listen to those who criticise you when you wobble. The key thing is it's a momentary wobble and then you get back on track. Always take it to the Father, because He is the Source who will help you to replenish and go again.

'Jesus said to him, "[You say to Me,] 'If You can?' All things are possible for the one who believes and trusts [in Me]!" Immediately the father of the boy cried out [with a desperate, piercing cry], saying, "I do believe; help [me overcome] my unbelief."'

Mark 9:23–24 (AMP)

DEVELOPING CHARACTER: FOUR SPIRITUAL MUSCLES

> *'And David said with longing, "Oh, that someone would give me a drink of the water from the well of Bethlehem, which is by the gate!" So the three mighty men broke through the camp of the Philistines, drew water from the well of Bethlehem that was by the gate, and took it and brought it to David. Nevertheless he would not drink it, but poured it out to the Lord. And he said, "Far be it from me, O Lord, that I should do this! Is this not the blood of the men who went in jeopardy of their lives?" Therefore he would not drink it.'*
>
> ***2 Samuel 23:15–16***

These things were done by three of David's mighty men. They didn't have to. They risked their lives for water! So, we have to ask, what was it about David's character that compelled these three mighty men to go on a potential suicide mission for him?

▶ Power or influence?

You can lead by power or by influence. The fundamental difference in how people respond to you is either because they have to (power) or because they want to (influence). Which are you? If people do it because they have to, they will do only what they have to and no more. This goes back to how you perceive others. Do you have a servant heart or a served heart?

Let's revisit 1 Samuel 24…

'Now it happened, when Saul had returned from following the Philistines, that it was told him, saying, "Take note! David is in the Wilderness of En Gedi." Then Saul took three thousand chosen men from all Israel, and went to seek David and his men on the Rocks of the Wild Goats. So he came to the sheepfolds by the road, where there was a cave; and Saul went in to attend to his needs. (David and his men were staying in the recesses of the cave.) Then the men of David said to him, "This is the day of which the Lord said to you, 'Behold, I will deliver your enemy into your hand, that you may do to him as it seems good to you.'" And David arose and secretly cut off a corner of Saul's robe. Now it happened afterward that David's heart troubled him because he had cut Saul's robe. And he said to his men, "The Lord forbid that I should do this thing to my master, the Lord's anointed, to stretch out my hand against him, seeing he is the anointed of the Lord." So David restrained his servants with these words, and did not allow them to rise against Saul. And Saul got up from the cave and went on his way.'

1 Samuel 24:1–7

Would you have killed Saul? Do you have the character to discern what was happening? Do you know that Saul behaved like an enemy but was actually a father figure? How do we know? Because David called him father and Saul called David son. But all the indicators pointed to enemy, but David's character and relationship with God were crucial for how he led.

God gives us many templates for developing our character and none is better than the others. I want to laser-focus on this one because it provides a template against which you can self-assess, get feedback from peers and those who work for you, and have clarity about what you must do. No one is exempt from developing character.

DEVELOPING CHARACTER: FOUR SPIRITUAL MUSCLES

> *'But also for this very reason, giving all diligence, add to your faith virtue, to virtue knowledge, to knowledge self-control, to self-control perseverance, to perseverance godliness, to godliness brotherly kindness, and to brotherly kindness love. For if these things are yours and abound, you will be neither barren nor unfruitful in the knowledge of our Lord Jesus Christ. For he who lacks these things is shortsighted, even to blindness, and has forgotten that he was cleansed from his old sins. Therefore, brethren, be even more diligent to make your call and election sure, for if you do these things you will never stumble; for so an entrance will be supplied to you abundantly into the everlasting kingdom of our Lord and Saviour Jesus Christ.'*
>
> ***2 Peter 1:5–11***

This Scripture identifies seven spiritual muscles that we must develop as entrepreneurs and business leaders:

- Virtue
- Knowledge
- Temperance (self-control)
- Patience
- Godliness
- Brotherly kindness
- Charity (love)

Before exploring the seven muscles, there is an emphasis on how we develop these muscles – with diligence, which is careful and persistent effort, and the earnest and persistent application to an undertaking. Note, however, the opposite of diligence is negligence. So, if you're not being diligent in your development, you are being negligent.

Diligence is an act and an attitude. It's about being careful with your thinking, words and actions. It's about being deliberate, as opposed to wishy-washy. You also need to be careful, attentive, deliberate and persistent. Becoming spiritually fit is the same as becoming physically fit; you've got to be intentional, and you've got to do the work.

The other thing we need to clarify is that all spiritual muscles are being added to your faith. This means you already have the foundation on which everything is being added. So let's explore these seven spiritual muscles. In this chapter, we will explore virtue, knowledge, temperance and patience.

▶ Add to your faith, virtue

Virtue is the inner strength to do the right thing, to make godly decisions. Virtue is an old word and a rare trait.

> *'Who can find a virtuous woman? For her price is far above rubies.'*
> **Proverbs 31:10**

Another description of virtue is fortitude. It's about building a wall of defence, developing your stickability and determination.

Examples of virtue

> *'I made a covenant with mine eyes; why then should I think upon a maid?'*
> **Job 31:1**
>
> *'I will set no wicked thing before mine eyes: I hate the work of them that turn aside; it shall not cleave to me.'*
> **Psalm 101:3**

'Love not the world, neither the things that are in the world. If any man love the world, the love of the Father is not in him. For all that is in the world, the lust of the flesh, and the lust of the eyes, and the pride of life, is not of the Father, but is of the world. And the world passeth away, and the lust thereof: but he that doeth the will of God abideth for ever.'
1 John 2:15–17 (KJV)

In all these examples there is a diligence, a strong conviction to do things in a godly way. What does this look like in the marketplace? Let's examine a few examples. Do you work on the Sabbath, when God instructs us to rest? Do you open business on a Sunday, because your competition is also open? But the Scriptures tell us we should ensure that our staff should also have rest.

Do you pursue a deal because the figures are compelling, but your gut is telling you, you shouldn't? Do you cut corners and deliver average solutions, when God requires us to have an excellent spirit? Do you treat your staff harshly, because the world sees people as resources, that you can rinse and discard?

Do an audit of the decisions you've made recently and ask yourself whether they are virtuous decisions. If they are not, then trust God enough to go back and rectify them.

A really important part of developing virtue is shifting how you think.

'Finally, brethren, whatsoever things are true, whatsoever things are honest, whatsoever things are just, whatsoever things are pure, whatsoever things are lovely, whatsoever things are of good report; if there be any virtue, and if there be any praise, think on these things.'
Philippians 4:8

There is a tendency to ponder on negative things. In business there may be a colleague or customer, who occupies your head – and not in a good way. There are challenges, suppliers letting you down, paying creditors, delivering on time, resolving customer complaints... It's easy to find yourself spiralling into negativity. But the Scriptures tell us to focus on good things. The energy this gives you is transformational and will help you to handle the hard stuff in a more composed and rational way.

For the readers of this book, Philippians 4:9 is equally important:

> *'Those things, which ye have both learned, and received, and heard, and seen in me, do: and the God of peace shall be with you.'*

So you need to think about who are you learning from. Who are your mentors and are they supporting you to grow spiritually and to build your business in a godly way? And who is learning from you? People are always watching you. Some are very obvious; the majority are not. What template are you given them? Is it clear that you and your business ventures stand out and glorify God, or can't they differentiate you from a worldly leader or worldly business?

The power of virtue is demonstrated in Daniel. He refused to bow down to King Darius, to the point that he was thrown into a lion's den and came out unscathed. Let's look at the impact of having virtue, an excellent spirit:

> *'Then this Daniel distinguished himself above the governors and satraps, because an excellent spirit was in him; and the king gave thought to setting him over the whole realm.'*
>
> **Daniel 6:3**

The result of having an excellent spirit was that the king considered putting a foreigner over his whole kingdom. Think about taking an outsider and putting him in charge of a kingdom. This is because such character couldn't be found among his own. When you mature in God, people will put you in places you could never imagine, simply because of how your relationship with God will transform you.

▶ Add to virtue, knowledge

"Talk no more so very proudly;
Let no arrogance come from your mouth,
For the Lord is the God of knowledge;
And by Him actions are weighed.'

1 Samuel 2:3

'The fear of the LORD is the beginning of knowledge, but fools despise wisdom and instruction.'

Proverbs 1:7

(Please note that 'fear' here means reverence.)

'When wisdom entereth into thine heart, and knowledge is pleasant unto thy soul; discretion shall preserve thee, understanding shall keep thee.'

Proverbs 2:10–11

'Receive my instruction, and not silver; and knowledge rather than choice gold.'

Proverbs 8:10

If you are going to fulfil your Dominion Mandate, you must be filled with knowledge. And just so there's no misunderstanding, by knowledge, I mean God's Word! So here are some important statements you need to consider:

- Knowledge is God's Word, which is TRUTH. Unequivocal and without negotiation. It is the acquaintance with facts, truths or principles.

- Wisdom is knowing how to apply knowledge to everyday situations.

- To develop your relationship with God, you must seek to understand God's thoughts.

If we need a template for adding knowledge, let's examine Solomon, the wisest man who has ever lived.

'Now, O LORD God, let thy promise unto David my father be established: for thou hast made me king over a people like the dust of the earth in multitude. Give me now wisdom and knowledge, that I may go out and come in before this people: for who can judge this thy people, that is so great? And God said to Solomon, Because this was in thine heart, and thou hast not asked riches, wealth, or honour, nor the life of thine enemies, neither yet hast asked long life; but hast asked wisdom and knowledge for thyself, that thou mayest judge my people, over whom I have made thee king: wisdom and knowledge is granted unto thee; and I will give thee riches, and wealth, and honour, such as none of the kings have had that have been before thee, neither shall there any after thee have the like.'

2 Chronicles 1:9–12 (KJV)

Just pause for a moment and reflect on your business. How impactful have you been to date? Think about the things you've asked for in prayer. When was the last time you asked for knowledge? Solomon sought to know God more, and because of that desire God honoured his request and gave him so much more.

The maturing Christian has to develop a discipline for God's Word. Link this to living the life of a disciple. Do not make it arduous. If you approach it with the right mindset, it is the most mind-blowing, life-giving experience you will ever have. You won't need to read another 10 Ways to Get Fit... or How to Get Rich in 50 Days. This is the most relevant business book, leadership manual, personal development Book ever written. It has every answer to every situation you will ever face, and it shows you how to handle things. So why isn't it at the forefront of your mind?

Joshua 1 shows us the power of knowledge:

> *'This Book of the Law shall not depart from your mouth, but you shall meditate in it day and night, that you may observe to do according to all that is written in it. For then you will make your way prosperous, and then you will have good success.'*
>
> **Joshua 1:8**

What's powerful about this word is that it tells us that if we meditate in the Word it will lead to prosperity and good success. But that means there is bad success too. Ignorance of the Word will lead to bad success, so readers, be alert, where are you gaining your knowledge from?

▶ Add to knowledge, temperance

Temperance is another term for self-control. This was my personal nemesis, and I believe I share this with many. Self-control is your capacity to restrain yourself, to control your emotions, desires or actions. It's impulse control.

Self-control is a cornerstone of discipline and hence a cornerstone of discipleship. Self-control is about taking authority over your thoughts, emotions and behaviours. It is crucial for the entrepreneur or business leader, because your behaviour shapes an organisation. It can heavily influence its success or failure.

If you remember the first word we focused on in this series was diligence. To maintain your relationship with God requires controlling your impulses.

'But the fruit of the [Holy] Spirit [the work which His presence within accomplishes] is love, joy (gladness), peace, patience (an even temper, forbearance), kindness, goodness (benevolence), faithfulness, gentleness (meekness, humility), self-control (self-restraint, continence). Against such things there is no law [that can bring a charge].'

Galatians 5:22–23 (AMP)

'Deliver my soul, O Lord, from lying lips and from a deceitful tongue.'

Psalm 120:2

The world's marketplace is driven by lies. The world is constantly deceiving its staff and its customers. The Volkswagen emissions scandal, also known as "Dieselgate", erupted in September 2015, when the United States Environmental Protection Agency (EPA) discovered that Volkswagen had installed illegal software, known as a "defeat device", into millions of its diesel vehicles to cheat emissions tests.

This software detected whenever the car was undergoing testing, and temporarily activated emissions controls to comply with regulatory standards. Under normal driving conditions, however, the vehicles emitted up to **40 times** the allowable levels of nitrogen oxides (NOx) – a harmful pollutant, linked to respiratory problems and environmental damage. The scandal led to a massive global recall of affected vehicles, significant fines, criminal charges against several Volkswagen executives, and a sharp decline in the company's reputation.

Volkswagen got caught, many haven't. We must stand out and have the discipline to tell the truth.

A core element of self-control is "No". It's saying "No" to feeling I've got to fit in; it's "No, I don't need to compromise myself to get the deal"; it's "No" to speaking negatively about a competitor.

Self-control means gaining a deeper knowledge of self. We think we know ourselves until we are tested. You look at your account, and you see figures you've never had in your life. You are able to buy things and go places you've always dreamed of. Can you show restraint? Can you tell yourself "Not yet"? Materialism will knock on your door. How important is what other people think of you?

Controlling our emotions is crucial because business will test every nerve you have. Staff will push you to the edge, emotionally. But self-control means you can control your upset, disappointment or anger and be thoughtful before responding.

If you know you are vulnerable in certain situations, then do not deliberately put yourself in them. Always remember the waterfall. Have you watched a film, where you have characters in some type of boat on a river? The scene starts off with a sense of calmness and tranquillity, with no cause for concern. However, without warning, the current becomes stronger, and the situation is no longer one in which they have control. Imagine you're in that boat, and as you approach the waterfall (and you will only know when it's too late), you are unable to fight against the current, and the rapids will send you over the edge.

We can find ourselves in situations, where we think we have everything under control, but without warning we're no longer in control and are being pulled over the edge. There are potential waterfalls for every one of us.

If you know what that river represents – the club, the bar, an old boyfriend or girlfriend – don't get into the river. Self-control means not placing yourself in a situation and testing yourself. Self-control is avoiding the situation in the first place.

The waterfall will make you feel bad, and you'll start feeling guilt and doubt about whether you're a Christian. That's what the devil wants you to do. He wants you to doubt that you're actually saved. So be honest with yourself.

Pastoral care is about helping you to develop. Don't feel you have to do it all by yourself. Ministers are there to help you overcome your struggles. All of us have our experiences and our experiences are designed to help you in your walk, as you will do with others in the future.

▶ Add to temperance, patience

The Greek word for patience is *hupomone* (hoop-om-on-ay) and it means **cheerful or hopeful endurance**. It's the capacity to accept or tolerate delay, trouble or suffering without getting angry or upset. It's the bearing of provocation, annoyance, misfortune or pain, without complaint, loss of temper, irritation, or the like.

The world is based on instant gratification, both personally and in business. That's why there is so much debt, that's why people seek highs in terms of drugs, alcohol and sex. That's why people steal. That's why many business owners run out and get houses and cars as trophies of success.

Let's link this back quickly to **Proverbs 21:5…**

'The plans of the diligent lead surely to plenty, but those of everyone who is hasty, surely to poverty.'

Diligence is not an instant thing; it takes time to develop. When you've made a mess of things, coming to Christ isn't going to rectify everything tomorrow. Scriptures have provided us with characters who help us to understand patience, especially when we've suffered hardships. David was anointed king as a teenager and yet endured much before sitting on the throne, and with Joseph I talk about his three Ps: the Pit, the Prison and the Palace.

Jesus' life was one that exemplified patience.

> *'For even Christ didn't live to please himself. As the Scriptures say, "The insults of those who insult you, O God, have fallen on me." Such things were written in the Scriptures long ago to teach us. And the Scriptures give us hope and encouragement as we wait patiently for God's promises to be fulfilled. May God, who gives this patience and encouragement, help you live in complete harmony with each other, as is fitting for followers of Christ Jesus.'*
> ***Romans 15:3–5 (NLT)***

The Amplified version tells us:

'For Christ did not please Himself [gave no thought to His own interests]; but, as it is written, The reproaches and abuses of those who reproached and abused you fell on Me. For whatever was thus written in former days was written for our instruction, that by [our steadfast and patient] endurance and the encouragement [drawn] from the Scriptures we might hold fast to and cherish hope. Now may the God Who gives the power of patient endurance (steadfastness) and Who supplies encouragement, grant you to live in such mutual harmony and such full sympathy with one another, in accord with Christ Jesus...'
Romans 15:3–5 (AMP)

'Now the ones that fell among thorns are those who, when they have heard, go out and are choked with cares, riches, and pleasures of life, and bring no fruit to maturity. But the ones that fell on the good ground are those who, having heard the word with a noble and good heart, keep it and bear fruit with patience.'
Luke 8:14–15

And not only that, but we also glory in tribulations, knowing that tribulation produces perseverance; and perseverance, character; and character, hope. Now hope does not disappoint, because the love of God has been poured out in our hearts by the Holy Spirit who was given to us.'
Romans 5:3–5

Business is full – full of trials and tribulations. There are many myths about instant riches. It is not to say you won't have an idea that's suddenly going to blow up, but if you consider nature, nothing in nature just blows up; there's a process. A common analogy we use is that a seed is buried and has to grow roots before anything breaks ground. So much in business is unseen and the process can take months or even years. That's why you must understand the Word, because it prepares you.

> '...knowing that the testing of your faith produces patience.'
>
> **James 1:3**

We don't know we have patience until it's tested. That's why we say: "Don't test my patience", because we lack it. Do we see the importance of being diligent in our speech? God will put you through some stuff to develop patience. The important thing to remember about patience is that it's hopeful or cheerful endurance. There's got to be something at the end of it.

Let's look at Jeremiah 18 and the Potter's House.

> 'Then I went down to the potter's house, and behold, he wrought a work on the wheels. And the vessel that he made of clay was marred in the hand of the potter: so he made it again another vessel, as seemed good to the potter to make it.'
>
> **Jeremiah 18:3–4**

It takes time to be created and fashioned by God. It takes time to develop a Kingdom business that brings glory to God. It's not an overnight thing. Think about how the potter would have taken his time to skilfully fashion the vessel. That's what God is doing with us and that's how we should approach the enterprises He has given us.

God's laws of nature require a seed to grow. Patience is required to be transformed from who you think are to who He says you are. A key part of patience is that we need to understand our purpose, and our purpose will exceed any sense of who we think we are. It takes time to prepare for destiny.

DEVELOPING CHARACTER: THE OTHER THREE SPIRITUAL MUSCLES

▶ **Add to perseverance, godliness**

> 'For physical training is of some value (useful for a little), but godliness (spiritual training) is useful and of value in everything and in every way, for it holds promise for the present life and also for the life which is to come.'
>
> *1 Timothy 4:8 (AMP)*

Godliness, the fifth muscle, is valued above physical fitness as it benefits this life and eternity. Derived from the Greek eusebeia, it means worship, respect, and reverence toward God.

Reverence is a childlike admiration, seeking to please with pure devotion. The closer your relationship with God, the deeper your reverence, marked by contentment in having God alone.

Godliness empowers you to revere people. When giving honour to a person, you hold that person in high regard and want to do what you can to support that person and do right by them. Note that reverence is not idolising. When you revere a person, you express an appreciation but never to the extent of placing them above God. If you idolise a person, it will be excessive and often mean placing them on a pedestal. Let's explore the application of godliness as an entrepreneur/business owner. When you have time, read 1 Timothy 6 in different versions. Here, I want to highlight some key verses.

> 'Let those who have believing masters not be disrespectful or scornful [to them] on the grounds that they are brothers [in Christ]; rather, they should serve [them all the better] because those who benefit by their kindly service are believers and beloved. Teach and urge these duties.'
>
> *1 Timothy 6:2 (AMPC)*

Scripture is teaching us that those who believe and work for you should make even greater effort, because you are of the faith, so that God may be glorified. Does your conduct facilitate or prohibit your staff from treating you in a respectful manner and from being willing to go the extra mile?

> *'And protracted wrangling and wearing discussion and perpetual friction among men who are corrupted in mind and bereft of the truth, who imagine that godliness or righteousness is a source of profit [a moneymaking business, a means of livelihood]. From such withdraw. [And it is, indeed, a source of immense profit, for] godliness accompanied with contentment (that contentment which is a sense of inward sufficiency) is great and abundant gain.'*
>
> **1 Timothy 6:5–6 (AMPC)**

Scripture shows us individuals who have a dubious character and perceive that godliness is a vehicle for generating money. This means that even those who are corrupt see the power and the value of godliness. But you should heed the Word and remove yourself from such people. Genuine godliness is described as a source of immense profit. It may not always translate into figures, but a reward is due you.

We then jump down to probably one of the most misquoted Scriptures:

> *'But those who crave to be rich fall into temptation and a snare and into many foolish (useless, godless) and hurtful desires that plunge men into ruin and destruction and miserable perishing.*
>
> *'For the love of money is a root of all evils; it is through this craving that some have been led astray and have wandered from the faith and pierced themselves through with many acute [mental] pangs.'*
>
> **1 Timothy 6:9–10 (AMPC)**

The love, the lust, the unrelenting passion for money is the root of all evils, not money itself. This means there is no evil, which is not linked directly or indirectly to the love of money. In business, the temptation will come at you from all directions. You will handle figures you can't fathom; be invited into social gatherings which you didn't know existed; be offered opportunities that are made unavailable to most people… That's why the next verses are so important.

'But as for you, O man of God, flee from all these things; aim at and pursue righteousness (right standing with God and true goodness), godliness (which is the loving fear of God and being Christlike), faith, love, steadfastness (patience), and gentleness of heart.'

1 Timothy 6:11 (AMPC)

▶ Add to godliness, brotherly kindness

The sixth muscle is brotherly kindness, and for some this may be uncharted territory. Some of us believe this is for church, but not for the workplace. Many of us believe we need to be tough, not show weakness in the workplace. But God requires different from us; we must be able to show genuine brotherly kindness.

'And again He entered Capernaum after some days, and it was heard that He was in the house. Immediately many gathered together, so that there was no longer room to receive them, not even near the door. And He preached the word to them. Then they came to Him, bringing a paralytic who was carried by four men. And when they could not come near Him because of the crowd, they uncovered the roof where He was. So when they had broken through, they let down the bed on which the paralytic was lying. When Jesus saw their faith, He said to the paralytic, "Son, your sins are forgiven you."'

Mark 2:1–5

What would this look like in your business in regard to one of your employees or peers? How would this manifest with customers or clients? There are many times, when I go to a business lunch with the intention of winning business, but the whole conversation is about Jesus. I'm sitting with senior leaders who just need that space to express their faith in ways they can't with others. I will gladly put down my initial intention, because that soul is a priority.

> 'Let love be without hypocrisy. Abhor what is evil. Cling to what is good. Be kindly affectionate to one another with brotherly love, in honour giving preference to one another…'
> **Romans 12:9–10**

The Amplified version says:

> 'Love is to be sincere and active [the real thing – without guile and hypocrisy]. Hate what is evil [detest all ungodliness, do not tolerate wickedness]; hold on tightly to what is good. Be devoted to one another with [authentic] brotherly affection [as members of one family], give preference to one another in honour…'
> **Romans 12:9–10 (AMP)**

Do your staff experience brotherly kindness, or do they experience sternness, coldness and distance? This is what many of us have observed or been taught. That's why Romans 12 begins with Paul pleading that we are not to copy the world, but we are to be transformed by the renewing of our minds. If you truly love your brother, then you will encourage, challenge, rebuke, hug, feed and clothe them. Brotherly kindness goes beyond our normal circumstances and circle of influence. It's not just family and friends. It's about genuine love for those who you don't know, for those you're not sure about. We must develop our desire and capacity for brotherly kindness and allow it to be who we are in the marketplace. Initially it will feel strange and uncomfortable, but trust God and see how your influence in your market will transform because you are applying His Word.

▶ Add to brotherly kindness, charity

The seventh muscle is also the greatest gift – love. So the first thing you may be asking is what is the difference between brotherly affection and love? It's important that you understand the fullness of love to know what is being expressed at different times.

In Greek, brotherly kindness is philadelphia – which is a fraternal affection, a love of the brethren. So this is the love you express to those you have close bonds with: your brothers and sisters in church; that group of friends you play sport with… there is a common bond.

You would think that this love is an easy love to express, but it's not, because people are people and many of those who you think have your best interest, don't. When you started that business and were working long hours, some of your friends were smiling in your face, but tearing you down and mocking you behind your back. But you are called to a higher level of thinking and conduct. You should be the one willing to go the extra mile for that person – even if you know they don't reciprocate. The love we are now talking about is *agapé* – unconditional love, the love God shows us daily.

> *'Though I speak with the tongues of men and of angels, but have not love, I have become sounding brass or a clanging cymbal. And though I have the gift of prophecy, and understand all mysteries and all knowledge, and though I have all faith, so that I could remove mountains, but have not love, I am nothing. And though I bestow all my goods to feed the poor, and though I give my body to be burned, but have not love, it profits me nothing. Love suffers long and is kind; love does not envy; love does not parade itself, is not puffed up; does not behave rudely, does not seek its own, is not provoked, thinks no evil; does not rejoice in iniquity, but rejoices in the truth; bears all things, believes all things, hopes all things, endures all things.'*
> *1 Corinthians 13:1–7*

I do not pretend this is easy and that's why I've described them as muscles you constantly need to exercise and develop. You're not going to see any changes taking place tomorrow or the next day, but over time, others will experience the love you show. At some point, you will look back and see how love has moulded your character, so that people see Jesus and not you.

So the big question is, what does this look like for you as a business leader and as an entrepreneur? Let's look at 1 Corinthians 13:4–7. Do you endure with people, as Christ has endured with you? Are you quick to let go of people? I have a colleague who many said I should have let go a long time ago, but I knew it wasn't about her work; it was about her soul. So I've laboured with her, and over time I've seen her grown. Has she accepted Jesus as her Lord and Saviour? Not yet. Does she bring me challenges? Yes! Is she an incredibly dedicated person? Yes, she is.

There is one statement I've been accused of on numerous occasions, and I truly am baffled by it: "You're too kind" or "You're too generous." Can someone help me decipher this? Please don't get me wrong, I am in no way perfect and there are probably many other things my team call me! But whenever I hear this, I actually rejoice, because I'm provoking my team to think about how we do business differently.

Are you puffed up? Do you flaunt your wealth in the faces of your staff? Do you talk about the places you eat and the clothes you wear more about the God you serve? Are you sensitive to the fact that some of your staff are potentially struggling with life? I'm not saying not to have nice things. I'm saying have perspective and simply recognise them for what they are – things. Easy come and easy go. Currently I'm driving a really desirable vehicle, but within a couple of days of acquiring it, I scratched it. I've kept the scratch there, to remind myself it's just a car!

Do you behave rudely? I don't think I need to say more but get feedback from those you trust. Ask them about how you show up. There are going to be times when your staff and your customers are going to get on your last nerve and push you to wanting to open your mouth to let them know what you really think. The Children of Israel pushed Moses to his limit, so it's likely you will have similar experiences. But these are a test. Pause, go away and pray, go for a walk, and praise, then come back with an intention to love them anyway.

These are a couple of examples, but go and reflect on these verses and be honest with yourself in terms of how do you measure up. And, where you fall short, be intentional about your prayer and your actions to change.

FULFILLING PURPOSE

Purpose has both universal and individual aspects. Entrepreneurs often focus intensely on their specific purpose, risking it becoming an idol. To prevent this, we must broaden our perspective and start by understanding our universal purpose, which applies to all believers.

> *'"Now this is the commandment, and these are the statutes and judgments which the Lord your God has commanded to teach you, that you may observe them in the land which you are crossing over to possess, that you may fear the Lord your God, to keep all His statutes and His commandments which I command you, you and your son and your grandson, all the days of your life, and that your days may be prolonged. Therefore hear, O Israel, and be careful to observe it, that it may be well with you, and that you may multiply greatly as the Lord God of your fathers has promised you – 'a land flowing with milk and honey.' Hear, O Israel: The Lord our God, the Lord is one! You shall love the Lord your God with all your heart, with all your soul, and with all your strength."'*
>
> **Deuteronomy 6:1–5**
>
> *Jesus said to him, "'You shall love the Lord your God with all your heart, with all your soul, and with all your mind.' This is the first and great commandment. And the second is like it: 'You shall love your neighbour as yourself.' On these two commandments hang all the Law and the Prophets."'*
>
> **Matthew 22:37–40**

Purpose is universal, and businesses should express love. Entrepreneurs solve problems, but true purpose elevates this to loving all—staff, customers, and stakeholders—without discrimination, as God commands.

I can imagine this statement has met with some resistance. If it has, good, we have to remember that the Gospel can offend, the Scriptures can grate on you and that's because we constantly need to be renewing our minds and ensuring that we desire to do everything in a Christlike way.

Each of us has a specific purpose, like David's kingship, Esther's mission to save a nation, or Paul's role in the salvation of the Gentiles. The question "What is my purpose?" is common to all, but remember, purpose isn't something we acquire—it is given by our heavenly Father. It is part of stewardship, where He delegates authority to us to fulfill His will.

Purpose isn't acquiring money or status – that is earthly – and I need to admonish you to be careful. They are traps which many Christian businesspeople have fallen into. They are by-products, benefits of your labour. Purpose is something much higher and much greater. Purpose will benefit mankind in ways which make money and power insignificant.

It's easy to be tempted by lucrative opportunities, but are they God-inspired? Is this what He has called you to do? Staying obedient to His purpose, even when other options seem more appealing, is key. Now that you know this, you're responsible for aligning your work with God's will.

I think Proverbs was written for entrepreneurs and business owners. It is loaded with wisdom that is illuminating and, when applied, game-changing. I want to bring a few to your attention regarding purpose.

> *'I, wisdom dwell with prudence, and find out knowledge of witty inventions.'*
>
> **Proverbs 8:12**

God is going to download to you witty inventions.

> *'A man's gift makes room for him, and brings him before great men.'*
> **Proverbs 18:16 (AMPC)**

Get this right, and your gifts will attract influential people to you. Focus on the inner three—relationship, character, and purpose—as they prepare you for the right opportunities.

BUILDING A POWERFUL TEAM

In this section, we want to look at how you create and build teams that will be able to dominate. We want your thinking to be disruptive, because God builds teams in very different ways to how the world does.

▶ Recruiting unusual suspects

> *'David therefore departed from there and escaped to the cave of Adullam. So when his brothers and all his father's house heard it, they went down there to him. And everyone who was in distress, everyone who was in debt, and everyone who was discontented gathered to him. So he became captain over them. And there were about four hundred men with him.'*
>
> **1 Samuel 22:1–2**

David recruited from those who were seemingly undesirable. They had no credentials and yet became mighty men of valour. Do we need to rethink how we build teams? What 1 Samuel 22 shows is that you can do extraordinary things with seemingly ordinary people.

I propose that the greatest team ever assembled was by Jesus in choosing His 12 disciples. The impact these 12 men had is still reverberating globally over 2,000 years later. No other team has that resumé. Now, when we look at the 12, they are common people, including four fishermen. But they also include Matthew – a tax collector – the most despised people in biblical times. Even worse, Jesus chose Judas.

> *'Then Jesus replied, "Have I not chosen you, the Twelve? Yet one of you is a devil!" (He meant Judas, the son of Simon Iscariot, who, though one of the Twelve, was later to betray him.)'*
>
> **John 6:70–71**

There was no individual of great reputation, no one highly educated. They were 12 ordinary men who yet, after a three-year apprenticeship, went on to achieve great things for the Kingdom. Jesus and David provide incredible templates for us when considering how to assemble teams. We should see more than other employers. The Holy Spirit should be invited into how we recruit. He knows the sheep and, more importantly, He knows the wolves.

> *'But the Lord said to Samuel, "Do not look at his appearance or at his physical stature, because I have refused him. For the Lord does not see as man sees; for man looks at the outward appearance, but the Lord looks at the heart."'*
>
> **1 Samuel 16:7**

Those who are least qualified and who outwardly don't seem to be a fit could be the actual person who will take your business to the next level. I'm not saying you should be reckless, but I am saying be prayerful; ask God to give you wisdom and be willing to go against what makes sense logically.

When talking about teams, we have to talk about leadership, because the success of a great team is heavily influenced by its leadership. Great leadership is not defined when things are going well; it's defined when your back is against the wall, when you're at your lowest point. So it also follows that great teams are defined in similar circumstances.

> *'"And now I urge you to take heart, for there will be no loss of life among you, but only of the ship. For there stood by me this night an angel of the God to whom I belong and whom I serve, saying, 'Do not be afraid, Paul; you must be brought before Caesar; and indeed God has granted you all those who sail with you.' Therefore take heart, men, for I believe God that it will be just as it was told me. However, we must run aground on a certain island."'*
>
> **Acts 27:22–26**

Equip them with purpose, the right systems and right equipment.

▶ Don't avoid Judas

The one person we actively avoid is Judas. Who wants a Judas, someone who you can't trust, someone who will betray you? I started to reflect on the Judases (plural) who have worked for me – and I've realised I've had a few. I've had one who forged my signature and took out a contract, which they didn't pay. I've had one who spread malicious lies about me and others; some who have tried to steal clients. The worst one was a Christian who took me to an employment tribunal, citing that I forced them to pray!

But, rather than focusing on how the betrayal hurt, I want you to understand that your Judas is a destiny enabler. No Judas, no kiss, no Cross, no Resurrection! Every Judas, despite the pain and the turmoil, has revealed something in my character – or in the business – that needed to be fixed. And, in some cases, their action has literally caused a chain reaction, which has led to incredible blessings.

You are never going to have a perfect team – it doesn't exist – so get comfortable with this, and comfortable with a Judas being on your payroll. The interesting thing is, if you are discerning, you will be able to identify who your Judas is, way before their act of betrayal. Your trust in God – that Judas must fulfil his role, so that you can fulfil purpose – is comforting.

▶ Wash their feet

I know that some of you are getting really nervous! I'm not saying to wash their feet literally, but what would washing your staff members' feet look like in your organisation?

> 'So when He had washed their feet, taken His garments, and sat down again, He said to them, "Do you know what I have done to you? You know what I have done to you? You call Me Teacher and Lord, and you say well, for so I am. If I then, your Lord and Teacher, have washed your feet, you also ought to wash one another's feet. For I have given you an example, that you should do as I have done to you."'
>
> **John 13:12–15**

There is so much for all of us to learn from this incredible act of service. The most important lesson for this book, however, is that He modelled servitude to His disciples. It was a very uncomfortable experience; Simon Peter refused and begged Jesus not to do so. Some of your staff will perceive you in a particular way and won't allow you to carry out something they see as being "below your status". But, if your identity is in Christ, you can push past their objections to serve in any capacity. Jesus said it very clearly: "I have given you an example, that you should do as I have done to you." What you model in your organisation will have a strong impact on the culture, the people and the outcomes. Modelling is humbling and may require vulnerability. It should come from a place of humility and never ego.

Servanthood leadership is the antithesis of most leadership models, which are represented by a triangle with the leadership at the top. Servanthood leadership flips the triangle, with the point at the bottom. It means you've not come to be served, but to serve. It means you have to be very intentional about where you are taking your team, what you want to do with them, and how you want them to show up. Servanthood leadership is impossible without love.

▶ What's love got to do with it?

The answer is everything. This is going to feel counterintuitive to what we have been taught and how we've conducted ourselves. But the commandments are explicit:

> *'Jesus said to him, "'You shall love the Lord your God with all your heart, with all your soul, and with all your mind.' This is the first and great commandment. And the second is like it: 'You shall love your neighbour as yourself.' On these two commandments hang all the Law and the Prophets."'*
>
> ***Matthew 22:37–40***

If ALL the Law and the Prophets hang on these two commandments, how can your business fall outside of them? And what does this look like in the marketplace?

Here are some things to consider:

- A genuine care for the welfare of all your staff. Let me be honest, I've not always got the balance right on this. For many years, I was more concerned about people's welfare to the detriment of individual performance, which impacted on the overall company performance. You've got to get the balance right.

- Do you know the names of your staff, their children? Do they feel able to share their struggles, knowing you will listen attentively?

- Acts of kindness – notice I didn't say random acts of kindness – should be part of your DNA.

One of my favourite TV moments is the Undercover Boss episode featuring Mitchell Modell, CEO of Modell's Sporting Goods. He was profoundly moved when he learned that an employee named Angel was living in a homeless shelter with her three children. This woman served in a way you would never believe; she had given a quality of service that few could match. In response, he promoted her to assistant manager, provided a $14,000 annual pay rise, and gifted her $250,000 (£185,000) to secure a new home for her and her family.

It breaks me every time I watch it because I've always said that I want to have the same impact on people, to truly change their lives. Always remember the souls you have immediate access to. That one act of kindness for a member of staff could literally lead them to salvation.

▶ ## Mentor, mentor, mentor

We should always be invested in our teams, and one of the most powerful forms of investment is mentoring. Jesus was a brilliant Mentor, so let's emulate Him. Sometimes we mentor the obvious – the people who are in our gaze and are clearly talented, or the ones who are bold enough to ask: "Please, would you mentor me?"

But stretch yourself and go beyond the norm to people who don't look like you, don't think like you, and definitely don't have the same life chances as you. Go into your organisation, ask the Holy Spirit to show you the person who needs your time and attention. And, for those mentees who don't know Christ yet, watch their intrigue about "Why me?" and "What drives you?" Trust me, they will see Christ in you and want to follow you.

▶ Then add a dose of purpose!

In my leadership workshops, I use the analogy of an orchestra. The purpose of an orchestra is to perform a symphony, derived from the Greek symphonia, meaning agreement. An orchestra is a group of people with different instruments creating harmony, all unified by a single purpose—clarity of purpose makes this possible.

Now, apply this analogy to your business. Is there a sense of agreement? Is there a clear script where everyone knows their part? When it comes together, is it a beautifully conducted symphony or just a noise? Are people simply playing their own scripts, because they've not been instructed what to play, or are they simply prefering to do their own thing? Most people in your organisation don't know why they are there!

Your Dominion Mandate cannot be achieved if your team/organisation doesn't have a clear sense of purpose. Nehemiah did it brilliantly after he had surveyed the broken walls of Jerusalem.

> *'Then I said to them, "You see the distress that we are in, how Jerusalem lies waste, and its gates are burned with fire. Come and let us build the wall of Jerusalem, that we may no longer be a reproach." And I told them of the hand of my God which had been good upon me, and also of the king's words that he had spoken to me. So they said, "Let us rise up and build." Then they set their hands to this good work.'*
> **Nehemiah 2:17–18**

The purpose was clear and the people responding accordingly. Give absolute clarity. I make it very clear to everyone who joins AKD, that it's more than a job; you're contributing to a mission and if you don't want to, that's OK, but you'd be better off elsewhere.

People want to belong to brilliant organisations that are purpose-driven and striving to do great things. People want to know their contribution matters. Reflect on how people show up to work for you; think about that amazing orchestra and be clear about the quality of sound you want to produce and what it currently sounds like.

DEVELOPING GREAT SYSTEMS

We could easily break this component of the Dominion Mandate into multiple chapters. Every enterprise is a matrix of systems, many of which we operate unconsciously. This isn't a bad thing if they are good and operating at a small level. But, because the Dominion Mandate is calling you to operate and function at a higher level, we have to be more conscious and more intentional about all the systems we have.

God is systematic. He planned. He created. He made provision. He developed. All these things required systems. Everything God does is deliberate and has purpose. In the Old Testament, He gave the people Leviticus – the laws and commandments on how the Children of Israel were to conduct themselves. Fundamentally, they were systems to provide order and ways to prosper.

▶ What is a system?

A system is an organised collection of interrelated components that function together to achieve a specific objective. These components can be physical, conceptual, or both, and they interact through defined processes and relationships. A system is characterised by its structure, boundaries, inputs, processes, outputs, and feedback mechanisms. It operates within an environment, which can influence and be influenced by the system's activities. Whether biological, mechanical, social or digital, a system's effectiveness depends on the coordinated functioning of its parts to produce the desired outcomes.

The quality of the systems you create will have a direct correlation on your productivity, profitability and impact. Poor systems will create waste and leakage; good systems will mitigate against this. You could have a company that, on the face of it, is doing well: you are acquiring lots of customers and delivering a great customer experience. But behind the scenes, invoices are going out late and you don't have a system for debt management. Just imagine customers taking 100 days to pay you, as opposed to your stated terms of 28 days. What is going to be the impact?

Systems constantly change. Years ago, there would be an administrator who would spend the first minutes of a day date-stamping the post and distributing it to the right people. Many of us rarely see a letter now, because modes of communication have changed.

There are many ways in which you can develop an overview of your systems. One way is to plot out the customer journey and to think about what is required at every touchpoint a customer (or potential customer) has with your business.

- Attracting potential customers
- Defining customer needs
- Converting customers
- Delivering the service
- Reviewing the service
- Retaining the customer
- Improving the service

Draw out a map and then describe every aspect of the customer journey with your team. In our business we have systems days, where we take time out to review different elements of the customer journey. This process involves:

- What happens before?
- What is the objective of this system?
- Who is involved?
- What are the key processes?
- What does 'great' look like?
- What are the risks and ways to mitigate?
- What happens if something goes wrong?
- What happens after?

I'm going to add one more crucial ingredient: does it give honour to God? We may think a system is insignificant to God, but everything works together – one system that gives you poor results will impact on another. We are called to function at a higher level than the world. Some entrepreneurs/business owners love this process, but many loathe it, because it requires attention to detail. There comes a time when you will not be available to get involved in granular details, but what you must do is create the culture where this work is embedded.

Do the same for the colleague experience. The quality of the customer experience is based on the quality of the colleague experience. The more they are invested into your organisation and brand, the more likely they will want to deliver a great service. So again, plot the employee journey from start to finish and identify every system. Determine how it will add value to the colleague and, as a result, add value to the customer and your organisation.

▶ Testing systems

You can have a system which on paper looks like a great system, but does it actually work? Does it give you the desired result? You've got to test it.

Quality Assurance: Despite delivering some brilliant work, my company had an Achilles heel for grammatical errors in our written work. It is something we had suffered from for years and was a real thorn in our side. These things are subtle but give very strong messages to our clients. So we had to fix it. You would think it was an easy fix, but it wasn't. Culturally it had become the norm, and despite many attempts we still had things going to clients with mistakes. So any system is only as good as the people operating it, and if they don't have pride in their work and in what they do, it's going to fail. Culture is everything in business, because that ultimately will be a big indicator to your success.

Mystery shoppers: Using mystery shoppers is a very simple way to understand your business through the lens of a customer. You can employ an agency, but to be honest, just having people you know test your business anonymously and provide you with detailed feedback is invaluable. Even better, when you have the scale, get your staff to mystery shop. This really helps to create a customer-centric approach amongst staff, because they are able to identify challenges and solutions for themselves.

Business continuity: COVID taught us that we are more agile and adaptable than we think. Many of us left five days in a workplace and suddenly found ourselves in very different working patterns. Whilst there is a lot of focus on planning, organisations need to also pay attention to preparedness.

Planning involves developing a structured, detailed approach to achieving specific goals, often relying on known variables and predefined steps. It's about creating a roadmap to guide actions based on anticipated scenarios.

In contrast, preparedness is about building the capacity to adapt when those plans inevitably face the unexpected. It focuses on cultivating flexibility, resourcefulness and resilience, enabling individuals and teams to respond effectively to unforeseen challenges or crises.

While planning provides a framework for action, preparedness ensures that when plans change or fail, there is still the ability to act swiftly, make decisions in ambiguity, and recover from setbacks.

So business continuity provides a blend of preparedness and planning. There will be disruption to business. We don't know when and we don't know what it's going to look like, but when it happens (and it will), we are ready for power outages, transport disruptions, pandemics, etc. Be ready today, because you just never know.

SEEKING A DIVINELY INSPIRED SOLUTION

The inner three pillars of the Dominion Mandate (relationship, character, purpose) are enablers for the three (team, systems, solutions).

Many people will start with the solution first, but in this model, it's the last element because, if you've developed the other five pillars, it will have an incredible impact on what you offer to the world.

A key part of "Go in and possess" is that this is an offensive stance, not a defensive one. So we have to understand how the solution you offer will fulfil your Dominion Mandate.

▶ It must add value

Anyone purchasing your solution should be able to see the intrinsic value of what you have to offer. Too many solutions are not really solutions, but ways to make money. At the heart of your business should be the desire to solve a genuine problem and add value to a person's life.

▶ Excellence

Excellence is often discussed in business but rarely achieved. Many businesses prioritize profits over quality, with boardrooms focused on increasing margins, sometimes at any cost—leaving excellence out of the equation.

Excellence has many components, including safety.

The crashes of Lion Air Flight 610 and Ethiopian Airlines Flight 302 were caused by a malfunction in the Boeing 737 MAX's MCAS system, triggered by faulty data from a single AOA sensor. The system's incorrect inputs led to loss of control in both incidents.

The crashes were further exacerbated by inadequate pilot training on the new system; poor communication between Boeing and the airlines; and insufficient regulatory oversight. These factors combined to cause the tragic loss of 346 lives and a subsequent global grounding of the 737 MAX fleet, highlighting significant flaws in Boeing's safety culture and regulatory compliance processes.

The development of the 737 MAX's MCAS system was driven by cost-cutting and competition, particularly with Airbus and its popular A320neo. To stay competitive, Boeing rushed to develop the 737 MAX for similar fuel efficiency and to maintain market share.

To save time and costs, Boeing modified the 737 design, adding larger engines that altered its aerodynamics. The MCAS system was introduced to address these changes.

Boeing made cost-driven decisions that compromised safety, including minimizing pilot training, not disclosing MCAS risks, and relying on a single sensor. These measures, aimed at reducing costs, played a key role in the crashes.

Even if your decisions aren't as large as Boeing's, be cautious. Cutting corners may seem justifiable, but God values safety and excellence. Trust Him to provide as you make the right choices.

▶ Truthfulness

> *'Differing weights are detestable and offensive to the Lord,*
> *And fraudulent scales are not good.'*
>
> **Proverbs 20:23 (AMP)**

God calls dishonest behavior an abomination, highlighting its serious consequences. While dishonesty is common in business, are you falling into the same trap?

While major scandals like 'Dieselgate' make headlines, many others go unnoticed. It starts small - will you always tell the truth to your customers, staff, and stakeholders? Manipulating numbers may seem insignificant, but your standards must align with God's, as your actions set the example for your staff.

If others will say or do anything to close a deal, look in the mirror first. Just as we teach children to tell the truth, in business, we must resist the temptation to manipulate it. The truth may cost in the short term, but God rewards those who reflect His character and will.

POSSESSING MEANS DISPOSSESSING

> *'But I will tarry in Ephesus until Pentecost. For a great and effective door has opened to me, and there are many adversaries.'*
> ***1 Corinthians 16:8–9***
>
> *'And about that time there arose a great commotion about the Way. For a certain man named Demetrius, a silversmith, who made silver shrines of Diana, brought no small profit to the craftsmen. He called them together with the workers of similar occupation, and said: "Men, you know that we have our prosperity by this trade. Moreover you see and hear that not only at Ephesus, but throughout almost all Asia, this Paul has persuaded and turned away many people, saying that they are not gods which are made with hands. So not only is this trade of ours in danger of falling into disrepute, but also the temple of the great goddess Diana may be despised and her magnificence destroyed, whom all Asia and the world worship."'*
> ***Act 19:23–27***

For some, this will be a hard chapter to read, because we may have a rose-tinted lens on what possessing means. Fundamental to the Dominion Mandate is possessing. And possessing for God means dispossessing the enemy!

First Corinthians 16:8–9 and Acts 19:23–27 are great illustrations of what the Dominion Mandate is for us. In 1 Corinthians, Paul talks about a great and effective door that has opened. This illustrates amazing opportunities for him to preach God's Word and win souls for the Kingdom. But with these great opportunities there will always be opposition. It's the same with us. We will achieve many great things in the marketplace: bringing great products and solutions to the market; delivering amazing customer experience, where genuine love is felt; witnessing to people just by how your business operates… You will be giving glory to God. BUT… there will always be opposition! And that opposition isn't going to relent.

In Acts we get a more vivid understanding of that opposition. Demetrius, a silversmith who makes his living off selling images of the goddess Diana, recognises that Paul and the 'Way' are a threat to his livelihood. So he calls the other silversmiths, who also profit from the same industry, not only to warn them of the impending danger, but to create a resistance. We will also experience our own Demetriuses, because possessing means we must dispossess them. We can't compromise; we can't apologise; we must possess. We must be used as a vehicle to give God glory.

On an individual level, you will have people in your life who just don't like you. They have neither rationale nor reason; they just can't stand you. The truth is, they are against the God you stand for because you are His ambassador. That will generate hate. Now take this from your personal experience and amplify it to your business that is shining for God.

The Dominion Mandate isn't for the faint-hearted who want an easy life. It requires a level of relationship with God and a commitment to His purpose that few have. We must be equipped to possess whilst experiencing adversities. And this is why the first three pillars of the Dominion Mandate – nurturing your relationship with God, developing your character, and fulfilling purpose – are crucial to ensure you have the capacity and resilience. The outer three (team, systems, solutions) are also important. You need to have a great team around you.

> *'So the whole city was filled with confusion, and rushed into the theatre with one accord, having seized Gaius and Aristarchus, Macedonians, Paul's travel companions. And when Paul wanted to go in to the people, the disciples would not allow him.'*
>
> **Acts 19:29–30**

If we go back to Acts 19, we see that Gaius and Aristarchus, members of Paul's team, were seized. They took a hit for the team and, when Paul wanted to go and intervene, other team members had to intervene and restrain him. Even while writing this book, we have had adversaries coming against us, and I have team members who have been taking the hits, but are still standing. So think carefully about who you have in your team, because they won't only be blessed by association, but will also be attacked by association!

So an important question is, do I have many adversaries? Do I have a Demetrius who is plotting against me, because I am possessing his market share? If you don't have one of these, then maybe you're playing it safe – in other words, maybe you're lukewarm!

The Dominion Mandate requires us to reflect and review how we think about and define what we do. As a business owner or entrepreneur, you will have worked incredibly hard, sacrificed so much, gone without sleep, etc. But all of this won't mean you have been successful; it won't mean you are fulfilling the Dominion Mandate God has given you.

At the beginning of 2024, God slapped me around the face. He told me I had believed the voices of people who were telling me about how successful I was. We had turned over £1,000,000 for the first time, and I had a real sense of achievement, only for God to tell me: "Don't kid yourself; this is mediocre." Many of us are living way below the promises God has for us. It's a hard truth, but a truth we have to accept, nonetheless.

▶ Go in and possess

> *"'See, I have set the land before you; go in and possess the land which the Lord swore to your fathers – to Abraham, Isaac, and Jacob – to give to them and their descendants after them.'"*
>
> **Deuteronomy 1:8**

Deuteronomy is an amazing book, in which Moses prepares the Children of Israel before they enter the Promised Land. Deuteronomy (from the Greek word deuteronómion) means 'second law' and, in fact, what it also means is repetition. God (through Moses) is preparing the Children of Israel by reminding them of the law, the commandments, the statutes they must follow, so that they can succeed and inherit all God has promised.

The first thing God does is remind them of the promise. The land of milk and honey has been promised. But to understand the power of this promise, we need to understand two key words – possess and sworn.

The Hebrew for possess is *yaresh* (yaw-raysh), which means to occupy (by driving out previous tenants and possessing in their place), to seize, to rob, to inherit, also to expel, to impoverish, to ruin, to cast out, to disinherit.

But it's important that we link the word possess with the word sworn. The Hebrew for sworn is *Shaba* (shaw-bah), which means to be complete. But Shaba *(7650 in Strong's Exhaustive Concordance)* is derived from Sheba (sheh-baw) which root is in seven. So it means making a declaration seven times. Seven means complete; it is a complete oath. So when God says: "The land which I have sworn to your fathers…", it means it is a complete and absolute declaration, an unbreakable promise.

Therefore, the promise is absolute, but we are required to possess. If the promise is absolute, why not just drop it into our laps? Why not simply give it to us without the struggle? As business owners and entrepreneurs, why do we have to experience such extraordinary levels of challenge, opposition and struggle?

A truth we need to embrace is that excellence is the result of pressure. Daniel, Esther and Joseph all experienced pressure, but they embraced and endured, and the squeezing produced excellence in character and in their achievements. When you embrace pressure, it develops your character. It enables you to understand the capacity and ability you have. Easy Street doesn't do that. Easy creates complacency and weak muscles, because there has been no test, no pressure. Easy creates laziness, a lack of awareness, and a lack of capacity.

Why do you think lottery millionaires often end up broke? Money was dropped into their lap. They didn't have to work for it; they weren't prepared for it; and there was a lack of appreciation for it. They may have been grateful, but that's different from appreciation.

Gratefulness is an emotional high: "I'm rich!" *Appreciating* it, however, means being cognisant of what has happened and what are the important decisions that have to be made. But, if you're not mature, you will be grateful but lack appreciation.

▶ What are your personal blockages?

There is an assumption that because you are a business leader or an entrepreneur your natural tendency is to possess. But, for many of some of us, there are blocks. These blocks could be personal, social or cultural, but they have an impact on us and therefore must have an impact on how we lead.

It's important that you can identify any personal blocks. Speak to friends and family, those who know you and seek their feedback.

Let's look at three principles of possessing.

▶ Possess what's yours

In Scripture, God was very clear what the Children of Israel were supposed to possess and what they were not allowed to touch.

> *"'And command the people, saying, 'You are about to pass through the territory of your brethren, the descendants of Esau, who live in Seir; and they will be afraid of you. Therefore watch yourselves carefully. Do not meddle with them, for I will not give you any of their land, no, not so much as one footstep, because I have given Mount Seir to Esau as a possession.'"'*
>
> **Deuteronomy 2:4–5**

Stop looking at what others have, it's not yours. Stop looking at the trajectory of others, the gifts of others, the blessings of others, they are not yours. Focus on what God has promised *you*. Be appreciative for what God has promised you and know that, when you possess what God has promised you, you will receive more than you could ever imagine.

If God has called you to dominate in catering, or in professional services, translations, whatever it is, *simply do it.* Souls exists *everywhere*.

When we lose focus and start looking at what others have, there are consequences. Firstly, there are consequences for the individual. In 2 Kings 5, we see the story of Elisha curing Naaman of leprosy in the presence of Elisha's servant, Gehazi. Naaman offered Elisha a gift to express his appreciation, but Elisha refused.

Let's see what Gehazi does.

'But Gehazi, the servant of Elisha, the man of God, said to himself, "My master should not have let this Aramean get away without accepting any of his gifts. As surely as the Lord lives, I will chase after him and get something from him." So Gehazi set off after Naaman.'

2 Kings 5:20 (NLT)

Gehazi chases after Naaman, tells a lie, receives a massive gift, returns and hides it from Elisha. But there are consequences for taking what's not yours…

'When he went in to his master, Elisha asked him, "Where have you been, Gehazi?"

"I haven't been anywhere," he replied. But Elisha asked him, "Don't you realise that I was there in spirit when Naaman stepped down from his chariot to meet you? Is this the time to receive money and clothing, olive groves and vineyards, sheep and cattle, and male and female servants? Because you have done this, you and your descendants will suffer from Naaman's leprosy forever." When Gehazi left the room, he was covered with leprosy; his skin was white as snow.'

2 Kings 5:25–27 (NLT)

But there are consequences for the collective, for your business. Beware of having a Gehazi or an Achan in your team. In Joshua, the Children of Israel had just captured and destroyed Jericho. Ai was next. It was much smaller and therefore should have been easily defeated. But the Children of Israel were defeated, because there was sin in the camp.

'But the Lord said to Joshua, "Get up! Why are you lying on your face like this? Israel has sinned and broken my covenant! They have

> stolen some of the things that I commanded must be set apart for me. And they have not only stolen them but have lied about it and hidden the things among their own belongings. That is why the Israelites are running from their enemies in defeat. For now Israel itself has been set apart for destruction. I will not remain with you any longer unless you destroy the things among you that were set apart for destruction.'
>
> **Joshua 7:10–12 (NLT)**

It was the sin, the greed of one man called Achan that caused a whole nation to be defeated. We must understand that what we do has an impact on others. This is often alien to us. We don't understand the impact of our behaviour beyond ourselves – some of us may stretch to thinking about our family, but that's it. We must understand that if we are knitted together and we are one body, then our individual actions have consequences on the collective. My actions have consequences on you and vice versa.

I recall a time, when a member of my team told a lie. The impact on him was he was dismissed; the impact on the team was we lost a lucrative opportunity, because the client decided the *whole organisation* couldn't be trusted.

We need to be honest about 'meism' – the tendency to focus on me, myself and I. Many of us bring 'meism' into both the Kingdom and also into our business ventures. You have to decide whether you really care about your brothers and sisters; whether you care about the souls that need salvation; or whether you are just fixated on yourself.

Normally business leaders understand the impact of their behaviour. But let's go deeper. It's not just those things you do in public; it's those private struggles too. If you are nice to your team, but horrible to your spouse or your children, or you're taking cocaine in your private club, do you *really* think that the consequences will be limited to yourself?

▶ Utterly destroy

One of our foundational statements is that our business ventures must be soul-winning vehicles. We are in the business of souls, and we have to be relentless.

Do you think the kingdom of darkness is going to say: "Here, take!"? No, it's a war.

Question: Just imagine that the enemy has got hold of your children and they are in desperate trouble. Which one of you would go into battle, with your head down, with a wimpish attitude, and say: "Please can I have my children back?" Of course not! *You're going to war.* And this means you have to utterly destroy.

I know that utterly destroy may be uncomfortable for some of you. For some of you, it may be triggering, conjuring up images of an angry and fearsome God. But stay with me, I want to explain to you why God says to "utterly destroy".

'"But of the cities of these peoples which the Lord your God gives you as an inheritance, you shall let nothing that breathes remain alive, but you shall utterly destroy them: the Hittite and the Amorite and the Canaanite and the Perizzite and the Hivite and the Jebusite, just as the Lord your God has commanded you, lest they teach you to do according to all their abominations which they have done for their gods, and you sin against the Lord your God."'

Deuteronomy 20:16–18

God knew why compromise in possessing the land was dangerous. The reason He commands to utterly destroy is because He understands the wickedness and the abominations of the enemy. He also understands the vulnerability and sinful nature of His people. So, to protect His people from sinning, He gives the instruction to utterly destroy. In business it's very easy to be seduced into doing things which are not consistent with Christ.

Let's get personal. Let's begin by utterly destroying every sin, that is imprisoning us. The only way we're going to break those habits, those addictions of sin, is by utterly destroying them. I want you to be brave, face the truth, and be relentless. If you compromise with sin, it's not going to stay in its corner; it's going to keep coming back. Suffocate everything that's stopping you.

From a business perspective, always act legally, but understand that as a soul-winning vehicle, you'll have enemies who won't play by your rules. To succeed, take market share from your competitors without pity, but offer a lifeline to their staff. True victory comes from putting God first, operating excellently, and showing love in all you do. Focus on your mission and souls, not your competition, and the results will follow.

'So it was, when they brought out those kings to Joshua, that Joshua called for all the men of Israel, and said to the captains of the men of war who went with him, "Come near, put your feet on the necks of these kings." And they drew near and put their feet on their necks. Then Joshua said to them, "Do not be afraid, nor be dismayed; be strong and of good courage, for thus the Lord will do to all your enemies against whom you fight."'

Joshua 10:24–25

I've prayed, "For what we're taking from our enemies, we give thanks," and I stand by it. In this Scripture, Joshua strengthens his captains' faith while defeating enemies. To fulfill the Dominion Mandate, you need a strong, aligned team. You don't have to only employ Christians, but be prayerful about key appointments and have people interceding for you. Be cautious of those who may disrupt your mission. I won't rest until you have yours.

▶ I don't rest until you have yours

'"Then I commanded you at that time, saying: 'The Lord your God has given you this land to possess. All you men of valour shall cross over armed before your brethren, the children of Israel. But your wives, your little ones, and your livestock (I know that you have much livestock) shall stay in your cities which I have given you, until the Lord has given rest to your brethren as to you, and they also possess the land which the Lord your God is giving them beyond the Jordan. Then each of you may return to his possession which I have given you.'"'

Deuteronomy 3:18–20

We must fight together, both within our organisations and with other Kingdom businesses. In our Dominion Mandate group, we support each other, sharing a passion for mutual success. The group will persist until everyone fulfills their mandate. Even when I've achieved my goals, I continue to support others—whether in business, prayer, or health—until they possess their land. We must care for others as much as ourselves, prepared to fight alongside them until they succeed. The Scriptures ask, "Is it time?" We must not seek rest before it's earned.

> *'Then the word of the Lord came by Haggai the prophet, saying, "Is it time for you yourselves to dwell in your panelled houses, and this temple to lie in ruins?" Now therefore, thus says the Lord of hosts: "Consider your ways! "You have sown much, and bring in little; you eat, but do not have enough; you drink, but you are not filled with drink; you clothe yourselves, but no one is warm; and he who earns wages, earns wages to put into a bag with holes." Thus says the Lord of hosts: "Consider your ways!"'*
>
> **Haggai 1:3–7**

One of the reasons you may be experiencing problems is because you've stopped fighting and are sitting in your panelled houses. God wants you to enjoy, but first we have got to possess.

Your enemies are not going to roll over; they are going to fight – and fight dirty. Initially they will ignore you because they will not see you as a serious threat. They may even laugh at you. But once they recognise that "Oh, these people are serious and they are threatening our market share", they are going to use any tactics possible to stop you. If you love Jesus, the world will hate you. Persecution is part of the process. People compromise because they don't want to be persecuted. As a business owner, love what God loves and hate what He hates. Hate no one but hate what they do and what they stand for. This is an important differentiation.

RELATIONSHIP WITH MONEY

Let's start with a few stats, which I would like you to visualise.

1. 1% of the world's population owns 43% of the world's wealth. Imagine a room with 100 people, one person would be standing and have possession of 43% of the wealth (Oxfam).

2. 50% of the world population own just 2% of the world's wealth. In the same room, half of you would stand up, but would only share 2% of the world's wealth (World Inequality Report, Oxfam).

3. As of 2024, approximately 8.5% of the world's population, or nearly 700 million people, are living on less than $2.15 per day – the threshold for extreme poverty used by the World Bank (Poverty, Prosperity, and Planet Report 2024, World Bank).

4. In the UK, around 14.4 million people live below the poverty line, representing approximately 21.6% of the population in 2023 (House of Commons Library).

5. In 2024, people in the UK owed a total of £1,864.9 billion in personal debt, which includes both secured and unsecured forms of borrowing. The average debt per adult is £34,612, and the average salary is £37,600 (Money Charity Report).

These are staggering stats, which most people are blind to. It's important to understand that the world economy is designed to benefit a few at the detriment of the majority. If we are citizens of God's Kingdom, we need to understand that Kingdom finances do not operate on the same model.

When you have a mandate to dominate, one of the things you are going to have to resolve is your relationship with wealth – and in particular with money. This is so important, because your understanding and relationship with money will either enhance you, advance the Kingdom or destroy you. The world may see success, but money could be eroding your soul.

We have to get to grips with this, because many of us don't have a healthy relationship with money and bring personal, warped thinking and bad habits into our entrepreneurial and business lives. In Numbers 13, people returned from spying the land with an 'evil' report. This led to generations dying in the wilderness, because they bought into false information. So what you think as a leader counts in all aspects of who you are and what you do.

So, before you read any further, quickly write down your relationship with money in three words. You will need this as you continue to read this chapter.

The Dominion Mandate is not about personal accumulation of wealth at the expense of others. It should be about the accumulation of wealth for others. We should not be comfortable with relative comfort for ourselves, whilst others are impoverished. It should bother us, it should agitate us. There should be a marked difference between a Kingdom business and a worldly business. We should shine for the right reasons, and one way to stand out should be the way in which we accumulate money; how we use it; and the impact we have.

Every year in our church we spend one month studying Kingdom finance, because we recognise its importance and the need to disrupt thinking and behaviours which believers bring in from the world. Kingdom finance is about how to acquire and utilise finances based upon Kingdom principles. This means for many of us we need to renew our minds.

From the outset, it's important to clarify that God has given us permission to get wealth.

> *'"And you shall remember the Lord your God, for it is He who gives you power to get wealth, that He may establish His covenant which He swore to your fathers, as it is this day."'*
>
> **Deuteronomy 8:18**

So God has given us the ability, capacity and permission to get wealth. But do we recognise this power? Do we utilise this power and what impact do we have with this power? In studying Kingdom finance there are three mindsets that govern our relationship with money. Which one do you identify with?

- The Poverty Mindset

- The Rich Mindset

- The Wealth Mindset

▶ The Poverty Mindset

A poverty mindset is a self-limiting, self-sabotaging thought process which inhibits growth in all dimensions of life. It ultimately blinds you to what is positive and possible. A poverty mindset is different from being poor. You may lack in areas of your life, but it doesn't mean you've bought into the circumstances. But a poverty mindset will limit and reduce your circumstances.

So what does the poverty mindset look like in Scripture?

> *'Go to the ant, you sluggard! Consider her ways and be wise, which, having no captain, overseer or ruler, provides her supplies in the summer, and gathers her food in the harvest. How long will you slumber, O sluggard? When will you rise from your sleep? A little sleep, a little slumber, a little folding of the hands to sleep – so shall your poverty come on you like a prowler, and your need like an armed man.'*
>
> ***Proverbs 6:6–11***
>
> *'He who has a slack hand becomes poor, but the hand of the diligent makes rich.'*
>
> ***Proverbs 10:4***
>
> *'I went by the field of the lazy man, and by the vineyard of the man devoid of understanding; and there it was, all overgrown with thorns; Its surface was covered with nettles; Its stone wall was broken down. When I saw it, I considered it well;*
>
> *I looked on it and received instruction: a little sleep, a little slumber, a little folding of the hands to rest; so shall your poverty come like a prowler, and your need like an armed man.'*
>
> ***Proverbs 24:30–34***

All three have a common denominator: laziness. Now some of you will be wondering who reading this book would be lazy. And yet, if you look at Proverbs 24, the writer observed the field of the lazy man and the vineyard of the man void of understanding. Both of them had assets and could therefore be deemed to be business people, just like you and me. Just because you have a business doesn't mean the poverty mindset doesn't apply.

▶ Esau had a poverty mindset!

> 'So the boys grew. And Esau was a skilful hunter, a man of the field; but Jacob was a mild man, dwelling in tents. And Isaac loved Esau because he ate of his game, but Rebekah loved Jacob. Now Jacob cooked a stew; and Esau came in from the field, and he was weary. And Esau said to Jacob, "Please feed me with that same red stew, for I am weary." Therefore his name was called Edom. But Jacob said, "Sell me your birthright as of this day." And Esau said, "Look, I am about to die; so what is this birthright to me?" Then Jacob said, "Swear to me as of this day." So he swore to him, and sold his birthright to Jacob. And Jacob gave Esau bread and stew of lentils; then he ate and drank, arose, and went his way. Thus Esau despised his birthright.'
>
> **Genesis 25:27–34**

I think one of the greatest illustrations of the poverty mindset is Esau.

Esau was the first-born and favoured by his father, Jacob. As the first-born, Esau automatically had a double portion of his father's inheritance. So you could say that Esau was set up. In addition, he was a skilful hunter. So he had a guaranteed inheritance and an occupation he was very good at. And yet for bread, stew and lentils, he gave up everything; he despised his inheritance. Why? Because he had a poverty mindset.

So what are the lessons we can learn from Esau?

- **He consumed everything today and left nothing for tomorrow.** Esau had come back from an unsuccessful hunting expedition. But he had no reserves, there was nothing preserved so that he could manage a difficult season.

RELATIONSHIP WITH MONEY

- **Esau had a microscopic lens.** Esau had a temporary problem: he was hungry.

- **Esau exaggerated the problem.** Esau was living in his father's household and there would have been provisions. His father was Jacob! And yet Esau was able to take a small temporary problem of weariness and hunger and conclude: "Look, I am about to die."

- **Esau didn't value what he had.** Esau had a double portion (66.7%) of his father's inheritance, which was huge:

> *'Then Isaac sowed in that land, and reaped in the same year a hundredfold; and the Lord blessed him. The man began to prosper, and continued prospering until he became very prosperous; for he had possessions of flocks and possessions of herds and a great number of servants. So the Philistines envied him.'*
>
> ***Genesis 26:12–14***

Esau had a vast inheritance, but didn't value it because he needed immediate gratification. If you don't value what you have, you will mistreat it, discard it, or despise it. That makes you vulnerable to those who understand and value what you have.

Esau was easily manipulated. Jacob was able to acquire his brother's birthright because he knew his brother was functioning from an emotional state rather than a rational state. He played him and won. It was the hunger and his emotions that were the real issue.

So please reflect and ask yourself: "Do I see any of myself in Esau?"

Recognising the poverty mindset

Here are a few indicators of a poverty mindset:

- You approach situations with a 'Woe is me' attitude.

- You have no discipline with money, as soon as you get it you spend it.

- You seek validation for what you have, rather than for who you are.
- Money occupies your thinking, but with no sense of purpose.
- You talk much but deliver little.
- You blame others for your circumstances.

▶ The Rich Mindset

A rich mindset is one which is driven to accumulate significant amounts of money. It is often accompanied by visible signs of expenditure. The wealth mindset is one where the means of making money could be questionable. A key feature of the rich mindset is that money can be made quickly – but lost equally as quickly.

'Achan replied, "It is true! I have sinned against the Lord, the God of Israel. This is what I have done: When I saw in the plunder a beautiful robe from Babylonia, two hundred shekels of silver and a bar of gold weighing fifty shekels, I coveted them and took them. They are hidden in the ground inside my tent, with the silver underneath...

'Joshua said, "Why have you brought this trouble on us? The Lord will bring trouble on you today." Then all Israel stoned him, and after they had stoned the rest, they burned them.'

Joshua 7:20–21, 25

'Then He spoke a parable to them, saying: "The ground of a certain rich man yielded plentifully. And he thought within himself, saying, 'What shall I do, since I have no room to store my crops?' So he said, 'I will do this: I will pull down my barns and build greater, and there I will store all my crops and my goods. And I will say to my soul, "Soul, you have many goods laid up for many years; take your ease; eat, drink, and be merry." But God said to him, 'Fool! This night your soul will be required of you; then whose will those things be which you have provided?' "So is he who lays up treasure for himself, and is not rich toward God."'

Luke 12:16–20

> *'But a certain man named Ananias, with Sapphira his wife, sold a possession. And he kept back part of the proceeds, his wife also being aware of it, and brought a certain part and laid it at the apostles' feet. But Peter said, "Ananias, why has Satan filled your heart to lie to the Holy Spirit and keep back part of the price of the land for yourself? While it remained, was it not your own? And after it was sold, was it not in your own control? Why have you conceived this thing in your heart? You have not lied to men but to God." Then Ananias, hearing these words, fell down and breathed his last.'*
>
> **Acts 5:1–5**

A rich mindset can be summarised in the following manner:

- You have a "me" heart.

- You have an unhealthy relationship with money. It rules you – it consumes your thinking and your actions.

- You are driven by selfish intentions for using money, aligned to personal goals and ambitions.

- You are materialistic – you tend to consider material possessions and physical comfort as more important than spiritual well-being.

The world promotes the "rich mindset," where people seek wealth without a real plan, often driven by a fear of returning to poverty. While no one wants to live poorly, this mindset can be dangerous. As shown in Scripture, the outcome of such a mindset can ultimately be death.

In 1 Samuel 25 we see the story of Nabal, who was described as very rich but also harsh and evil in all his doings. David asked a simple request of some provisions for him and his men, but Nabal – who had more than enough to share – was dismissive of David and his men. It was only because of his wife Abigail that David was restrained from killing Nabal for how he had treated him. Fast forward, after Abigail had intervened and appeased David and offered him provisions, she returned home to find her husband feasting "like a king" and drunk. So it was, in the morning, when the wine had gone from Nabal, and his wife had told him these things, that his heart died within him, and he became like a stone. Then it happened, after about ten days, that the Lord struck Nabal, and he died (1 Samuel 25:37).

The rich mindset often leads to spiritual death, as highlighted in Scripture, which is frequently misquoted in Timothy.

>
> *'Now godliness with contentment is great gain. For we brought nothing into this world, and it is certain we can carry nothing out. And having food and clothing, with these we shall be content. But those who desire to be rich fall into temptation and a snare, and into many foolish and harmful lusts which drown men in destruction and perdition. For the love of money is a root of all kinds of evil, for which some have strayed from the faith in their greediness, and pierced themselves through with many sorrows.'*
>
> *1 Timothy 6:6–10*

This message is crucial because we'll face many temptations and be exposed to experiences, people, and opportunities that others won't. You may be invited into circles that can change your life and business, but at a cost.

I was once stuck in a "rich mindset," driven by success and outward validation, even though I was still going to church and tithing. But my need for validation led me to live a life that looked enviable, until it wasn't.

Money is tempting, and there will be people who are attracted not to you, but to what you have. This can lead to choices that jeopardize everything. You might find yourself desiring things you never thought you needed, like £5,000 bags instead of £50 ones.

There's nothing wrong with material possessions, but what's driving you? The warning is clear: greed can lead to sorrow. Be honest with yourself about what motivates you and what could potentially ruin you.

▶ The Wealth Mindset

>
> *'A good man leaves an inheritance to his children's children, but the wealth of the sinner is stored up for the righteous.'*
>
> ***Proverbs 13:22***

> *'There is one who scatters, yet increases more; and there is one who withholds more than is right, but it leads to poverty. The generous soul will be made rich, and he who waters will also be watered himself. The people will curse him who withholds grain, but blessing will be on the head of him who sells it.'*
>
> ***Proverbs 11:24–26***
>
> *'Now it happened one day that Elisha went to Shunem, where there was a notable woman, and she persuaded him to eat some food. So it was, as often as he passed by, he would turn in there to eat some food. And she said to her husband, "Look now, I know that this is a holy man of God, who passes by us regularly. Please, let us make a small upper room on the wall; and let us put a bed for him there, and a table and a chair and a lampstand; so it will be, whenever he comes to us, he can turn in there."'*
>
> ***2 Kings 4:8–10***
>
> *'Now the multitude of those who believed were of one heart and one soul; neither did anyone say that any of the things he possessed was his own, but they had all things in common. And with great power the apostles gave witness to the resurrection of the Lord Jesus. And great grace was upon them all. Nor was there anyone among them who lacked; for all who were possessors of lands or houses sold them, and brought the proceeds of the things that were sold, and laid them at the apostles' feet; and they distributed to each as anyone had need.'*
>
> ***Acts 4:32–35***

The wealth mindset focuses on holistic, long-term financial fulfillment, creating systems for sustainable, generational success. It's driven by assets rather than effort and is less visible.

So the key features of the wealth mindset include:

- The heart of stewardship
- A capacity to generate wealth
- A healthy relationship with money, where you are in charge of money and not vice versa

- Clear intentions for using wealth, which is aligned to God's will

- Selfless, charitable

Entrepreneurs with a wealth mindset see their purpose as creating a soul-winning vehicle, using their success to transform lives. They act quickly and generously, which allows God to bless them with more.

I've experienced all three mindsets—wealth, rich, and poverty. While I've been grounded in the wealth mindset, the poverty mindset often tries to tempt me. God has tested me with finances, and I'm mindful not to fail those tests.

I once sat on the board of a charity for domestic violence victims when the Holy Spirit told me, "Give Raj all your money." I froze, questioning if it was God, but I knew it was. After thinking of my son, with whom I had a business deal, I called him, apologized, and told him what God had instructed. I returned to the meeting, asked Raj for her bank details, and transferred all the money. I left with peace, though it made no sense.

I share this to encourage Kingdom business leaders: we will be tested to operate by Kingdom principles, not the world's. Acts 4 offers a beautiful illustration of how those with a wealth mindset should operate.

> *'Nor was there anyone among them who lacked; for all who were possessors of lands or houses sold them, and brought the proceeds of the things that were sold.'*
>
> ***Acts 4:34***

Whenever this is taught or preached, I love watching how people begin to shuffle in their seats! But let me point out ***'...those who were possessors of lands or houses'***, plural. They didn't sell the house or land they dwelt in, they sold assets. Their motivation for selling assets was to ensure that no one among them lacked. I pray we see this as a model of how we will function in the marketplace.

Operating in a wealth mindset, for many of us, will require letting go of the past. Growing up with nothing is a major driver for many of us and no one wants to be poor. But having escaped a poverty mindset, the rich mindset will trap many of us, because now that we have money, we may find ourselves in unfamiliar territory. If you are not rooted in God and in your faith, this dilemma can literally kill you.

The wealth mindset is rooted in stewardship, focusing on responsibility, accountability, adding value, and being rewarded. It requires faith, discipline, and a shift from spending to investing—across multiple levels:

- Investing in your relationship with God to truly be guided by His will.

- Investing in educating yourself. You must be financially literate to handle big figures.

- Investing in assets. Assets are not going to give you a return today or tomorrow, but in due time, that sacrifice is going to provide you a reward.

- Investing in people, a major part of being wealthy are the people and relationships you have. Do they love being around you? Are they excited to hear what you have to say, or do they mute their voices when you enter the room?

And to conclude, I want to look at David, who started as a shepherd and was even overlooked by his own father! I want to show the infectious nature of someone with a wealth mindset…

> 'Furthermore King David said to all the assembly: "My son Solomon, whom alone God has chosen, is young and inexperienced; and the work is great, because the temple is not for man but for the Lord God. Now for the house of my God I have prepared with all my might: gold for things to be made of gold, silver for things of silver, bronze for things of bronze, iron for things of iron, wood for things of wood, onyx stones, stones to be set, glistening stones of various colours, all kinds of precious stones, and marble slabs in abundance.
>
> 'Moreover, because I have set my affection on the house of my God, I have given to the house of my God, over and above all that I have prepared for the holy house, my own special treasure of gold and silver: three thousand talents of gold, of the gold of Ophir, and seven thousand talents of refined silver, to overlay the walls of the houses; the gold for things of gold and the silver for things of silver, and for all kinds of work to be done by the hands of craftsmen. Who then is willing

> *to consecrate himself this day to the Lord?"*
>
> *'Then the leaders of the fathers' houses, leaders of the tribes of Israel, the captains of thousands and of hundreds, with the officers over the king's work, offered willingly. They gave for the work of the house of God five thousand talents and ten thousand darics of gold, ten thousand talents of silver, eighteen thousand talents of bronze, and one hundred thousand talents of iron. And whoever had precious stones gave them to the treasury of the house of the Lord, into the hand of Jehiel the Gershonite. Then the people rejoiced, for they had offered willingly, because with a loyal heart they had offered willingly to the Lord; and King David also rejoiced greatly.'*
>
> 1 Chronicles 29:1–9

God wants to bless you with a lot. The question is, are you ready?

▶ Practical steps towards a wealth mindset

I want to conclude this chapter with practical steps you can make to help you shift to the wealth mindset.

- **Pray** – pray for a change of heart, pray to let go of the past, pray for wisdom and understanding, pray that God will equip you to be ready to handle all He has for you.

- **Study** – the Scriptures are loaded with stories that show us the different mindsets. Meditate on the Scriptures in this chapter as a start.

- **Stop spending** – cut out those unnecessary expenses, personally and in your business. Every company has waste, identify it and eliminate it.

- **Budget** – again, personally and for the business. Become disciplined with a budget. You will find it transformational.

- **Become financially literate** – learning is a lifelong process, so no one is void of learning more and being able to apply more lessons and strategies to what you do.

- **Coach/mentor** – you may want to find someone specifically to help you navigate becoming financial literate and competent.

TAKE CARE OF YOURSELF

There is a significant danger in overworking in the pursuit of dominion, especially when we become so focused on success that we lose sight of God's intentions for us. The Bible clearly warns against both overworking and the underlying motivations that drive us to push ourselves beyond healthy limits. Overworking can often stem from a desire for control, recognition, or wealth, which can distract us from God's purpose. The Scriptures remind us that work is important, but it should not consume us or become an idol. We must ensure our efforts are aligned with God's will, not driven by our own ambitions or worldly pressures.

To stay aligned with God, it's essential to maintain a strong sense of self-awareness. We must constantly evaluate whether our actions, decisions, and work ethic reflect His calling for our lives.

▶ Know yourself

> *'When you sit down to eat with a ruler, consider carefully what is before you; and put a knife to your throat If you are a man given to appetite. Do not desire his delicacies, for they are deceptive food. Do not overwork to be rich; because of your own understanding, cease! Will you set your eyes on that which is not? For riches certainly make themselves wings; they fly away like an eagle toward heaven.'*
> **Proverbs 23:1–5**

Business brings many temptations, and I've personally faced the consequences. I didn't literally put a knife to my throat, but I lost everything—except my family and God. I was consumed by envy, trying to live a champagne life on lemonade money, always comparing myself to others. I worked tirelessly, relentlessly pursuing wealth, but I got burned badly because I was chasing a worldly definition of success. The cost of my mistakes was high, but I thank God for the trials I endured. Through those difficult moments, He showed me His way, teaching me true fulfillment and the importance of aligning with His purpose.

▶ Don't try and do it all yourself

> *'And so it was, on the next day, that Moses sat to judge the people; and the people stood before Moses from morning until evening. So when Moses' father-in-law saw all that he did for the people, he said, "What is this thing that you are doing for the people? Why do you alone sit, and all the people stand before you from morning until evening?" And Moses said to his father-in-law, "Because the people come to me to inquire of God. When they have a difficulty, they come to me, and I judge between one and another; and I make known the statutes of God and His laws." So Moses' father-in-law said to him, "The thing that you do is not good. Both you and these people who are with you will surely wear yourselves out. For this thing is too much for you; you are not able to perform it by yourself.'*
>
> ***Exodus 18:13–18***

Entrepreneurs, especially in the early stages of a business, can often fall into the trap of hoarding responsibilities, trying to do everything themselves. In the beginning, multitasking is necessary, but the danger comes when this mindset continues past the startup phase. If you remain stuck in this cycle, it can become a lifelong habit, preventing growth and delegating responsibilities effectively. I've learned this firsthand, as I still struggle with letting go of certain tasks. Holding onto too much creates burnout and limits the potential of both the business and the individuals around you. It's essential to recognize when it's time to delegate and trust others, allowing for sustainable growth and aligning with God's purpose for the business.

We need to be careful of overworking, and taking on everyone else's work. "They don't do it as well as I want", "It's quicker to do it myself"… these and many other statements are used to justify, but they are often excuses and smokescreens for something deeper: not being willing or not trusting others to let go. Listen to Jethro. The thing you do is not good – both you and these people who are with you will surely wear yourselves out. Think how demoralising it must be for talented people in your organisation to be held back, because you won't let go. I want you to envisage a conductor of an orchestra. Have you ever seen them leave their rostrum, take an instrument from one of the musicians and start to play? So let go and let them!

▶ Rest

Rest is crucial. It is one of the ten commandments – and that should settle any argument.

> *'"Remember the Sabbath day, to keep it holy. Six days you shall labour and do all your work, but the seventh day is the Sabbath of the Lord your God. In it you shall do no work: you, nor your son, nor your daughter, nor your male servant, nor your female servant, nor your cattle, nor your stranger who is within your gates. For in six days the Lord made the heavens and the earth, the sea, and all that is in them, and rested the seventh day. Therefore the Lord blessed the Sabbath day and hallowed it."'*
>
> ***Exodus 20:8–11***

But the Sabbath has been diluted and is broken by many of us. I used to work every Sunday after church because "there was so much to do". I was then convicted by hearing a sermon about the Sabbath and I knew I had to change. So I didn't work on a Sunday until 11pm, thinking I would get a pass! But I just made up my mind to honour God's work and stop working on a Sunday. I told my team, and it was liberating.

Breaking this commandment is often driven by fear. Fear of not working hard enough, fear of not meeting financial targets, fear of failure. But for God it's demonstrating a lack of trust – we don't trust Him to fulfil His Word. Or we are chasing something that doesn't have God in it. Whatever reason you have, it's missing the mark.

> *'There remains therefore a rest for the people of God. For he who has entered His rest has himself also ceased from his works as God did from His.'*
>
> ***Hebrews 4:9–10***

If your life and business are truly centered on God, you will make the conscious decision to rest on the seventh day, following His command for Sabbath rest. This practice isn't just a physical need but a spiritual one, designed to help you recharge and reconnect with God. Just as physical muscles need rest to grow stronger, so does your spirit and your business.

It's important to remember that muscles don't grow during the workout itself, but rather in the recovery phase. When you exercise, you create small tears in the muscle fibers. These tears need time to repair, and during this repair process, the muscles become stronger and more resilient. Similarly, in business, when you allow yourself the time to step back and rest, you're creating space for growth and renewal. Rest isn't just an interruption; it's a vital part of the process that allows you to come back with more energy, focus, and creativity. By resting, you're not only refueling physically but also strengthening your purpose, vision, and ability to serve in alignment with God's plan.

Rest is not just a physical necessity but also a divine principle that God instituted for our well-being. When you rest, you align with His rhythms, trusting that He is in control of your business and your life. Just as muscles grow through rest and recovery, your mind, body, and spirit thrive when you give yourself permission to pause, recharge, and reflect. This time of rest allows you to hear God's guidance more clearly, renew your creativity, and come back with a stronger sense of purpose, ultimately leading to greater success in both your personal and professional life.

EXIT STRATEGY: BEWARE

A lot of emphasis is placed on having an exit strategy when you start your business. Often the world will encourage us to have a plan to exit after a period of time for a certain amount of money. I was always uncomfortable with this when discussing with my contemporaries. In my mind I always felt that creating a business should be something generational that you pass on to the family. And I still believe this.

In my consultancy work, I was deeply impacted by the story of C&A that was started by Clemens and August Brenninkmeijer in 1841 and has stayed in the family ever since. What struck me was that the values of the family, which are rooted in Christianity, have been maintained over generations. There are deep expectations of humility and service that are ingrained into family members and how they conduct themselves. And they created a hugely successful business which dominated clothing retail in the 1980s and '90s.

But there was something deeper that I was missing and in prayer God gave me the revelation. You have worked tirelessly to create a business that is thriving and doing great things in the marketplace. Clearly this will become an attractive proposition for someone to come and offer you a figure. They see the potential that this will add to their portfolio, or the potential of revenue that you've not seen. The figures you will be offered will be hugely attractive, potentially life-changing. Who wouldn't want to cash in and live happily ever after? But we have to go back to our foundation. We are creating soul-winning vehicles. We are creating enterprises that bring glory to God in the marketplace.

If you sell to someone who doesn't have the same faith AND motivations as you, you've just given up all the territory that you possessed. You have limited the Dominion Mandate to one generation. Be careful that you don't sell to the enemy; they will be zealous about purchasing your territory.

'"You shall make no covenant with them, nor with their gods. They shall not dwell in your land, lest they make you sin against Me. For if you serve their gods, it will surely be a snare to you."'

Exodus 23:32–33

We have to be honest and recognise: 1) we are mortal and there is a limit to our time running an enterprise, and 2) we will be able to take it only so far and then others should be in a position to build upon what we've created.

The Dominion Mandate should continue past you. Just like a church, if it dies when the pastor dies, there is something fundamentally wrong in how the leadership have functioned.

Who is your Joshua? Who is your Elisha? Both went on to do greater works than their masters. We should have the same mindset and develop leaders with the same heart and passion for the Dominion Mandate. Paul spent time pouring into and developing leaders to continue the work. His writings to Timothy and Titus are especially poignant. We must do the same.

But we must be comfortable recognising that our future leaders will have a different part of the Mandate to fulfil, probably bigger and better than ours. Don't hinder them. Don't try to impose an old wineskin mindset on them, because they will be receiving new wine, and we know what happens if we mix the two – loss of both.

FINAL THOUGHTS

The Dominion Mandate excites me and scares me at the same time. I'm in awe that God gave me this to steward and I feel the weight of responsibility. I don't write this from a place of knowing it all and having got it all together; I'm writing during the toughest year in business I've ever had. I actually reflected on how we made it through! But it was tough not because of market conditions or the wars or high inflation. It was tough because God was pruning me. Pruning isn't easy, but it's necessary if we are going to grow in a way that glorifies God.

I sincerely believe there is a Dominion Mandate for those whose businesses are God-inspired – a mandate to dominate, to shine brightly in the marketplace, to win souls, and to show the world what happens when you submit everything to our heavenly Father.

Is it easy? No. The mantle we take up is not for the faint-hearted, the lazy or the lukewarm. It is for the Esthers, the Jobs, the Davids, the Josephs, the Shunammite women, the Calebs and, of course, the Joshuas.

Read and pray. Ask the Holy Spirit to give you direction on how to possess the land that is yours. Do so with joy, do so with faith, knowing that your heavenly Father will never leave you nor forsake you.

You were born to have dominion, so go forth and do it!

'The Lord bless you and keep you;

The Lord make His face shine upon you,

And be gracious to you;

The Lord lift up His countenance upon you,

And give you peace.'

Numbers 6:24–26

DOMINION MANDATE

AUTHOR PAGE

Akin has been blessed in a number of different roles. He had a distinguished career, working in local government, where his initial passion was working with young people who were (or at risk of being) in care or with youth involved in anti-social behaviour. He later moved into more strategic roles, holding senior management positions in social care.

One day, he had an epiphany and walked out of his job.

Since then, he has been an entrepreneur and has undertaken many ventures – some great and some less so! An encounter with God transformed everything, including his approach to entrepreneurism and business. He is dedicated to supporting Christians in the marketplace, and God has called him to steward the Dominion Mandate.

Akin is CEO of AKD Solutions Ltd – an international organisational change consultancy whose mission is to stimulate brilliance in individuals, teams and organisations. Much of his time is spent with senior leaders from different industries and from across the world, providing solutions to major corporate problems. He is regarded as a creative and a disrupter.

Akin is also an elder in his local church, ARC South. Most importantly, he is married to his incredible wife and is blessed with two children.

The Dominion Mandate is his first book.

www.ingramcontent.com/pod-product-compliance
Lightning Source LLC
Chambersburg PA
CBHW041504010526
44118CB00001B/13